Peanuts and Philosophy

T0151844

Popular Culture and Philosophy® Series Editor: George A. Reisch

For full details of all Popular Culture and Philosophy® books, visit www.opencourtbooks.com.

Popular Culture and Philosophy®

Peanuts and Philosophy

*You're a Wise Man,
Charlie Brown!*

EDITED BY
RICHARD GREENE AND
RACHEL ROBISON-GREENE

OPEN COURT
Chicago

Volume 106 in the series, Popular Culture and Philosophy®, edited by George A. Reisch

To find out more about Open Court books, call toll-free 1-800-815-2280, or visit our website at www.opencourtbooks.com.

Open Court Publishing Company is a division of Carus Publishing Company, dba Cricket Media.

Copyright © 2017 by Carus Publishing Company, dba Cricket Media

First printing 2017

Printed and bound in the United States of America.

Peanuts and Philosophy: You're a Wise Man, Charlie Brown!

ISBN: 978-0-8126-9948-7

Library of Congress Control Number: 2016954617

This book is also available as an e-book.

For Susan Robison

When we say Schulz is a Poet, we say it chiefly as a challenge, to take a stand. The declaration "Schulz is a poet" amounts to saying "We love Charlie M. Schulz unconditionally, intensely, fiercely, intolerantly; and we will allow no debate, and anyone who disagrees is either a villain or an illiterate."

—UMBERTO ECO, "The World of Charlie Brown," p. 36

Contents

Contents

Thanks

Working on this project has been a pleasure, in no small part because of the many fine folks who have assisted us along the way. In particular, a debt of gratitude is owed to David Ramsay Steele and George Reisch at Open Court, and Charles Schulz (of course!), the contributors to this volume, and our respective academic departments at UMass Amherst and Weber State University.

Finally, we'd like to thank those family members, students, friends, and colleagues with whom we've had fruitful and rewarding conversations on various aspects of all things *Peanuts* as it relates to philosophical themes.

It Was a Dark and Philosophical Night

It was a dark and stormy night. It was the night before Snoopy's big dogfight with the Bloody Red Baron. The setting was a sidewalk café in Paris, the Sopwith Camel was parked outback, and inside the soda pop was flowing.

All the greats were there: Socrates, Plato, Aristotle, Descartes, Hume, Nietzsche, Freud, Wittgenstein, Sartre, the World War One flying ace (and his little yellow bird), the kid with the blanket, the psychiatrist, the classical pianist, the really dusty kid, the Little Red-Haired Girl, the little girl in love with the kid with the blanket, and of course, good ol' Charlie Brown.

They had gathered to discuss many things, each of which was of the greatest philosophical significance, but most of all they were there to discuss life (war tends to bring out the big topics). It's tough being a kid, but the *Peanuts* gang has all the philosophers they need to sort out important issues pertaining to the meaning of Christmas, kite-eating trees, the Great Pumpkin, baseball, dating, critical thinking, induction, existence, happiness, virtue, friendship, ethics, and aesthetics.

Join these seventeen brave philosophers as they delve into the philosophical themes in the world of *Peanuts*. It's a journey that promises to have more twists and turns than a "to the death" air-battle with the Bloody Red Baron, more excitement than a kiss on the cheek from the Little Red-Haired

Girl, and ultimately more satisfaction than a football kicked squarely through the uprights (or just kicked at all).

These grown-ups have quite a bit to say, even if to the kids it all sounds like "Mwaa mwaa mwaa!"

I

Happiness Is a Warm Existence

1
Charlie's Eternal Quest for the Little Red-Haired Girl

WIELAND SCHWANEBECK

"The One That Got Away" is a staple in popular culture: frequently quoted in nostalgic movies, young adult fiction, and pop songs, mused over by nostalgic protagonists—usually male ones.

In Judd Apatow's comedy *Funny People* (2009), a stand-up comic quips that it's mostly "guys and serial killers" who mourn for "The One Who Got Away." There may be some truth in that: the ones who lament their missed romantic opportunities are not only anti-heroes but to some degree also anti-social, and the reason *she* got away often is that *he* either didn't find the courage or lacked the social skills and status to come clear about his feelings.

No one represents this dilemma better than Charlie Brown, who is always longing for the Little Red-Haired Girl. She made her first *Peanuts* appearance—though 'appearance' may be the wrong word—in 1961, at a time when the United States (and arguably the rest of the world, too) entered a new period in cultural history.

This was the year of John F. Kennedy's inauguration as President of the United States, the year of a number of key events in Cold War history (including the Bay of Pigs invasion), and of Kennedy's announcing the Apollo program—the goal of which was to have a man on the moon by the end of the decade.

As Charlie Brown walks on the playground on November 19th 1961, he seems quite unaware of what is going on in the rest of the world. Perhaps the deserted playground around him is a sign that his fellow young Americans are busy following current events, or they might be just making a point of excluding Charlie from their games—given Charlie's notoriously low status amongst his peers, the latter scenario seems more likely. After all, Schulz had established the character of Charlie Brown in the very first *Peanuts* strip (October 2nd 1950) with two children seeing him and commenting: "Good ol' Charlie Brown. How I hate him!"

Over the next few panels of the 1961 strip, Charlie begins to reflect on the misery of his solitary lunch hours, wondering why no one ever invites him to sit with them, why his mother prepares him the same peanut-butter sandwich every day, and why she always includes a banana in his lunch-box: "I guess she means well."

In a monologue that would not feel out of place in a Samuel Beckett play (as with so many speech contributions in Schulz's comics), Charlie also ponders the quality of the paint job which has been done on the bench he is sitting on. He stares off into the distance, at "that little girl with the red hair"—the phrase indicates that he has seen her before. She is not a newcomer but seems to have been around forever. Unlike other characters like Linus, Rerun, or Sally (whose 'births' Schulz's readers were allowed to witness before they quickly grew up to become younger siblings with distinct personalities of their own, stuck in the perpetual youth of all of Schulz's creations), the Little Red-Haired Girl appears out of the blue, yet at the same time, she's identified as a permanent fixture in Charlie's universe— no formal introductions necessary.

The first strip featuring the Little Red-Haired Girl already lays down the rules for all of her future non-appearances: we are not privy to Charlie's point-of-view and thus never get a glimpse of her, at least not in Schulz's own drawings. She features in some of the movies, though, including *You're in Love, Charlie Brown* (1967), and *It's Your First Kiss, Charlie Brown* (1977).

As Charlie muses that the Little Red-Haired Girl might be a good runner, a smile creeps across his face (the only one in this whole Sunday strip, which consists of fourteen slim panels), and when the bell rings, he shuffles off, glumly staring into the face of another "two-thousand, one-hundred and twenty" lunch hours, presumably before he graduates from high school.

In hindsight, the first appearance of the Little Red-Haired Girl indicates a prophetic stroke on Schulz's part: Charlie's life-long obsession and permanent unfulfilled romantic interest arrives in the *Peanuts* world at about the same time as the United States (with Kennedy's inauguration) enters the most fruitful, eventful, and revolutionary decade of the postwar era.

This was a time where everything and everyone seemed to be in permanent transition:

> black civil rights; youth culture and trend-setting by young people; idealism, protest, and rebellion; the triumph of popular music based on Afro-American models and the emergence of this music as a universal language . . . the search for inspiration in the religions of the Orient; massive changes in personal relationships and sexual behavior; a general audacity and frankness in books and in the media . . . the new feminism; gay liberation; the emergence of "the underground" and "the counterculture"; optimism and genuine faith in the dawning of a better world. (Arthur Marwick, *The Sixties*, p. 3)

By the end of the decade, the nation was not the same anymore, yet some of the most ground-breaking cultural achievements of this "mini-renaissance" were already starting to fade from memory, the decade's initial optimistic spirit having given way to the pessimism and national crisis of confidence of the 1970s.

Moving Away

In July 1969 Schulz spins a whole two-week narrative arc around how Charlie loses the Little Red-Haired Girl: he notices that moving vans have stopped in front of her house and draws the correct conclusions. Linus begins to give Charlie an emphatic pep talk, trying to inject him with some confidence to finally go up and talk to her. Charlie, once more living up to his well-deserved reputation as "wishy-washy" (Lucy), prefers screaming ("Aaugh!") to actually doing something, and he spends several of the following strips summing up his regrets: that he never really talked to the Little Red-Haired Girl when he had the chance and that he mistakenly thought he had all the time in the world.

"I thought I could wait until the sixth-grade swim party or the seventh-grade class party," he cries, "or I thought I could ask her to the senior prom." Charlie's reaction when Linus informs him he has to say good-bye now ("I've never even said *hello* to her!") betrays wit, yet it is also perfectly useless. The moving vans leave, as does the station wagon with the Little Red-Haired Girl in it, which leads even Linus, that most Zen-like free-spirit of the whole *Peanuts* universe, to finally lose his calm: "You never do anything! All you ever do is just stand there! You drive everybody crazy, Charlie Brown!"

Having been kicked by his friend for indulging in even more daydreams about the Little Red-Haired Girl, Charlie continues to stare at the empty house as the sun goes down, and it's only the mundane reality of having to feed his dog which gets him out of his rut: "I have lots of sentimentality," Snoopy resonates in his typically wry and completely unapologetic manner, "it's my stomach that's practical."

With the departure of the Little Red-Haired Girl, Schulz seems to close the book on the whole decade and its unfulfilled utopias. The 'Summer of Love' was all but a distant memory then, for the signs of the time seemed to signal the end of an era: it was the year when the Beatles gave their last public performance (on top of the Apple Records building in London) and effectively ceased to work together as a band, the year when the Charles Manson gang murdered actress Sharon Tate, and when massive protests erupted against the United States' increased involvement in Vietnam, following

Nixon's televised address to the nation in which he called out to the "silent majority" to support American troops.

The singular moment of collective strength in that year was represented by Neil Armstrong's setting foot on the moon on July 20th 1969. The day of the moon landing marks the exact mid-point in Schulz's two-week story on the Little Red-Haired Girl's departure. On the following day (July 21st), the moon can be glimpsed behind Charlie, who is still staring catatonically at the empty house and clearly does not take any notice of one of the twentieth century's most iconic moments.

Charlie's Obscure Object of Desire

For the readers of *Peanuts*, the Little Red-Haired Girl provides only one of many story-arcs which recur regularly over the years, next to staples like Snoopy's hunt for the Red Baron, Lucy's efforts to get dedicated pianist Schroeder to notice her, or Sally's on-going quarrel with the school building.

Charlie's distant longing differs from most of these other arcs in that it is derived from one of the most recognizable master-plots in all of story-telling: the quest narrative, though its downbeat ending (or rather: lack of ending) makes for a quite different final act than we're used to. Whereas the hero in a classical quest narrative pursues the object of his desire through various trials and tribulations so as to be rewarded in the end (be it with the Holy Grail, one ring to rule them all, or the Ark of the Covenant), Charlie's quest is characterized by perpetual disappointment and lack of initiative.

As a true existential hero, Charlie is no more capable of getting up and doing something about his misery than Beckett's heroes Vladimir and Estragon in *Waiting for Godot* (1953) who, in the last lines of the play, voice their willingness to finally leave ("Well? Shall we go?"—"Yes, let's go."), only to remain exactly where they are until the curtain comes down.

However, *Peanuts* readers would be disappointed if this were in any way different—the lack of closure is exactly the prerequisite of Charlie's Sisyphean ordeal, which makes him a true existentialist. Albert Camus, in his *Myth of Sisyphus* (the book which comes closest to being an existentialist manifesto), points to Sisyphus as an example humankind should follow. Having repeatedly incurred the wrath of the gods because of his deceitfulness, Sisyphus is sentenced to perform the same pointless task over and over again: to roll a rock to the top of a mountain, only to see it roll down again. He knows that the effort itself is "futile and hopeless," yet it is his determination in the face of his pointless existence which makes him an "absurd hero" (pp. 88–89).

Like Sisyphus, Charlie Brown seems forever destined to remain an unlucky schlub; he heads the world's most useless baseball team, he's disrespected by his dog, and he can never stop Lucy from pulling away the football at the last moment. The Little Red-Haired Girl is Charlie's permanent object of desire—ironically, her leaving town in the station wagon changes nothing about this.

As 'the one who got away', she continues to prey on his mind in Schulz's comics, and she makes occasional guest appearances throughout the following years, her radiant beauty and Schulz's continued insistence that she remain invisible (save for one 1998 strip when the Little Red-Haired Girl can be seen in silhouette, dancing with Snoopy) adding to her aura, emphasizing that she is not quite of this world.

Having met her during her summer vacation, Peppermint Patty, who denigrates herself as "a mud fence" and as a mere "plain Jane," admits that the Little Red-Haired Girl (whom Patty mistakenly assumes to be a rival for Charlie's affection) "just sort of sparkles." This comment aligns her even further with the treasured object that usually marks the goal of the quest narrative and puts her outside the realm of ordinary flesh-and-blood human beings.

Tragically, though, Charlie's lack of courage will forever prevent him from finding out that the Little Red-Haired Girl, too, errs, curses, sweats, and belches. Instead, he prefers to idealize her from afar. No wonder, then, that Charlie is amazed to find a pencil with her teeth marks on it: "She nibbles on her pencil . . . She's human!"

The Color of Danger

At the same time, Charlie's decision to keep his distance may point to an implicit fear of the Little Red-Haired Girl: redheads are frequently associated with being more libidinous and aggressive than people with blonde or brown hair. Popular culture, history, and cultural memory offer a whole gallery of redheads, none of which can be adequately described as "little girls."

Queen Elizabeth I, the traitors and adulterers featured in fables and fairy-tales, and some of the most iconic femme fatales of the Rita Hayworth variety are anything but little and girlish. The cautionary tales surrounding these women suggest to the male spectator that it might be better to steer clear of them (Junkerjürgen, *Hair Color*, pp. 228–233).

Charlie Brown may just have a rough idea that the Little Red-Haired Girl will swallow him whole—while Schulz's comics never suggest that she's dangerous or malevolent, it's interesting to note that the color red also marks another character in the *Peanuts* universe who never materializes: the Red Baron, Snoopy's nemesis when he's moonlighting as the World War I Flying Ace, the flying Moby-Dick to Snoopy's airborne Captain Ahab.

Neither the Red Baron nor the Little Red-Haired Girl ever appears in person, causing the reader to wonder whether they only exist in the imagination of the daydreaming protagonists, and they effectively serve as the story's MacGuffin—a term popularized by Alfred Hitchcock to designate the highly elusive object of desire that propelled his plots. In Hitchcock's spy movies, the MacGuffin provides the reason that we have a plot on our hands to begin with: it can be a stolen microfilm, the blueprint of a secret military weapon, or a non-existent spy created as a decoy (as in 1959's *North by Northwest*).

In the case of *Peanuts*, the MacGuffin takes various forms, including that of Snoopy's archenemy and of Charlie's love interest—when he does not have his baseball team on his mind, it is the Little Red-Haired Girl who keeps him going and inspires his musings; no wonder that she had her heyday during the 1960s Cold War hysteria, when Hitchcock-inspired spy capers of the 007 variety suggested to audiences that all the excitement was in the chase itself and that the goal was nothing.

The same is true of desire. The psychoanalytic school of literary theory has put forward the idea that it is desire which keeps us hooked on a story, as desire is *the* driving force of the narrative. Characters move through a story because they lack something, and they want to compensate for this lack. In the reading process, desire occurs on at least two levels: "Narratives both tell of desire—typically present some story of desire—and arouse and make use of desire as dynamic of signification" (Peter Brooks, *Reading for the Plot*, p. 37).

Psychoanalytic theory is usually quick to link desire to the realm of the libido, but it actually extends to ambition and the formation of identity, as is the case in classical novels of education or contemporary coming-of-age tales. Charlie Brown may not be the most obvious choice as protagonist for either of those (he is, after all, stuck in the limbo of permanent childhood and neither ages, learns, nor arrives anywhere), but he certainly experiences the essence of what psychoanalysts like Jacques Lacan understand as desire: the wish to be recognized by the Other, and that which sits between two demands, "the demand for the satisfaction of need and the demand for love" (*Seminar, Book V*).

Crucially, it is doomed to remain unsatisfiable, for the subject's desire aspires towards a phantasmagoria which has little to do with the real object, the relationship between the two remaining "phantastical in its essence"—a point very much emphasized by Schulz's refusal to have the Little Red-Haired Girl materialize, which coincides with Charlie's subconscious wish not to endanger his idealized version of her.

In one strip from the 1980s, he observes her house from behind a wintry tree to which his mittens have become frozen—even if this wasn't the case, we can be sure that Charlie would invent another reason to remain in hiding. It was a point pretty much lost on the makers of 2015's *Peanuts Movie*, at the heart of which resides a fundamental misunderstanding not only of the *Peanuts* philosophy, but also of the Little Red-Haired Girl's relevance for the *Peanuts* universe.

Peanuts Betrayed

The Peanuts Movie, the first feature-length adaptation of Schulz's work in more than thirty years, was released in 2015 to coincide with the sixty-fifth anniversary of the original daily strip. Though its animations are quite impressive and do a good job of subtly updating Schulz's two-dimensional drawings to contemporary 3D animation standard (whilst retaining his original, sparse style for some dream sequences and thought-bubbles), the movie alienated quite a few dedicated fans of the comics, especially those who cherish the *Peanuts* universe for its refusal to sugar-coat hard truths.

Plot-wise, the movie is a rather generic piece that drives home the same points as so many other run-of-the-mill animated films aimed at young children. Its key propositions boil down to mere truisms: "To thine own self be true", believe in your dreams, stand up for yourself, yada-yada-yada. At least parts of this philosophy sit rather uneasily with the agenda of Schulz's strips, which clearly emphasize existential gloom and the inevitability of failure over the spirit of 'onwards and upwards,' as so many other chapters in this volume can testify. The conventional movie plot usually suggests that 'thinking big' pays off, but there's a reason that Charlie Brown and the others are known as 'peanuts': They're all too aware of their limits and frequently get reminded of them.

Admittedly, it may be nigh impossible to picture a ninety-minute film which both does justice to the conventions of Hollywood entertainment *and* stays true to Schulz's philosophical vision of gloom and despair. What works in Schulz's four-panel strip doesn't translate easily into a feature-length film, which is why so many of the screenwriters' decisions go against the essence of the *Peanuts* philosophy.

Not only do they turn the hunt for the Red Baron into a series of elaborate chase sequences and add a female love interest for Snoopy, they also have Charlie inject himself with lessons in confidence, the first one of which tellingly says, "Forget everything you ever knew about yourself."

It's a statement which equally applies to the transformation Schulz's character undergoes here, for the filmmakers infuse him with the 'Ragged Dick' spirit of persistence and entrepreneurial fervor. *This* Charlie Brown, driven by his wish to "show them you're a winner" and that he is "not a quitter," accomplishes the task of finishing Tolstoy's *War and Peace* over the weekend (and writes a magnificent book report on it), he makes a noble sacrifice for his little sister during a talent show, and he even acts as a mentor to a younger boy when he teaches him how to fly a kite—victories which Schulz's character could only have dreamed of, or which he could only have achieved under a different name (as in the famous 'Mr. Sack' storyline from 1973).

It's as if somebody took Arthur Miller's *Death of a Salesman* (1949) and substituted its final act for an epilogue in which Willy Loman wins the lottery and the family makes up over milk and cookies.

The same goes for many of the other *Peanuts* characters: Here, Linus neither seeks solace in his own pagan cult surrounding the Great Pumpkin, nor does he quote apocalyptic prophecies from the Bible, preferring to deliver fortune cookie wisdoms like "It's the courage to continue that counts," spurring his friend Charlie on. On the surface, this mantra may seem true to the spirit of the *Peanuts* universe—for isn't the necessity to continue what the publication history of the strip emphasizes, what with its fifty-year run of daily stories?

On closer inspection: not really. The ethos of Schulz's never-ending story has less to do with the conviction that the ordeal will inevitably lead to triumph, and more with the Sisyphean spirit I've sketched above: Charlie is a truly absurd hero who keeps rolling his rock come what may, and Schulz's dedication over half a century of work certainly mirrors Charlie's attitude in the face of 2,120 lunch-hours to come. *His* Charlie Brown carries on not because of an innate conviction that there will be ample reward and that all obstacles can be overcome, but because the only alternative—suicide—would amount to "acceptance at its extreme", against which absurd man's only possible attitude is the defiant spirit of "day-to-day revolt." In Beckett's oft-quoted phrase: "I can't go on, you must go on, I'll go on" (*Three Novels*, pp. 407).

The movie's misreading extends to the treatment of the Little Red-Haired Girl: the final scene reveals her to the audience, following the kind of striptease logic applied in monster films like *Jaws* (1975)—the film initially just teases her presence in order to gradually reveal more of her, and full disclosure (the 'money-shot', as it were) is reserved for the final act. Clearly, the idea is to get her down to earth, so as to bring her within Charlie's reach. On finding the pencil with her teeth marks, he no longer wonders that she is human (as he did in the comic strip), but he rather celebrates the fact that "we have something in common."

Moreover, by turning Charlie into an unlikely hero and allowing him to earn the Little Red-Haired Girl's kiss in the final scene (cue Linus: "It must feel pretty great to be Charlie Brown right now"), the film provides a degree of romantic closure, thus implicitly admitting to an unsolvable conundrum. Whereas the endless continuity of Schulz's strip *required* the Little Red-Haired Girl never to appear in person so as to keep Charlie's desire in permanent suspension, the movie (by virtue of the obligatory three-act structure) insists on putting a final stop to Charlie's quest, bending to the conventions of the happy ending.

Yet delivering Sisyphus from his ordeal in essence kills everything that's admirable about him. Giving flesh and blood to the Little Red-Haired Girl and presenting Charlie Brown with what he wants may just be the worst thing anyone could do for him.[1]

---

[1] This chapter is for Kathy and Stefan.

2
3eanuts and the Existential Schulz

DANIEL LEONARD

One fine day, Lucy holds the football and Charlie Brown kicks it.

Meanwhile, a publisher offers to buy Snoopy's novel. Linus overcomes his blanket addiction and meets the Great Pumpkin. Peppermint Patty gets an A. Spike discovers a friend nearby in the desert, Woodstock finds his mother on Mother's Day, and all Charlie's absent valentines from years past come flooding in.

Loves are requited: Lucy's for Schroeder, Sally's for Linus, and Charlie's for the Little Red-Haired Girl. To top it off, the baseball team scores one homer after another and Charlie pitches a perfect game to win the Little League World Series.

What then?

Do they all walk off happily into the sunset, their defining struggles resolved, their lives complete? Do they live in dread of fresh letdowns? Do they find new reasons to be unhappy? Is such a scenario even imaginable in their world? In ours?

Peanuts is full of disappointments, rejections, and uncertainties without any permanent relief in sight. What's more, the characters don't seem able to change; Charlie Brown's wishy-washyness, Lucy's fussbudgeting, and Linus's insecurity are there to stay. Even in childhood, they find themselves unsatisfying people thrown into an unsatisfying world.

What are they to do? This is the question of existentialism.

Existenschulzism in a Peanut Shell

Existentialism first became popular in Europe after World War II. Since the Industrial Revolution, many had believed human civilization was on a path of boundless progress in all aspects of society and technology. But humanity's new-found heights of knowledge—the secrets of the atom—and of culture—the refined attitudes of modernity—led instead to destruction, tyranny, and death on an unforeseen scale. If splitting atoms destroys cities, maybe nature isn't on our side; maybe the universe is indifferent to us. And if even the most sophisticated system of values leads to bigotry and violence, maybe all hard-and-fast value systems are doomed to fail.

Whether it's science, religion, or philosophy that lets us down, we can find ourselves affirming the title of Linus's 1960 Great Pumpkin memoir, which "tells what happens to an innocent child when his faith in something is destroyed": *My Belief Was Rudely Clobbered.*

And if we simply seek a new foundation elsewhere, we have to deal with Linus's reply to Lucy eight years later, when she proclaims that all the answers to life lie on the other side of a nearby hill: maybe another kid is on the other side, thinking the same thing.

What Linus is implying sounds almost like relativism, which holds that the foundations which offer absolute answers to the big questions aren't mutually exclusive and all may have some truth in their context. But his point is that *none* of the foundations has those answers—so maybe Lucy should try different questions.

Suppose it's true that we have no pre-established place in the big scheme of things and there are no clear universal principles to judge our behavior. Is there anything left for "meaning" to mean? Historically, philosophers have tended to study the nature or essence of humanity as a whole, then to apply what they learn about this nature to individuals;

they work from the top down, defining the category to reach truths about its members.

But existentialists point out that there is no eternal, constant human nature—and even if there were, not every person puts every human possibility in action. Instead, human nature is dynamic; it forms from the bottom up, becoming what the group of individuals who live at a given time decide to do with themselves. So the traditional script is flipped and, as existentialist philosopher Jean-Paul Sartre (1905–1980) writes, "Existence precedes essence." So, we exist before we exist *for* anything. The existentialist says: Meaning is what we make it.

The "-ism" of "existentialism" is a bit of a misnomer. Existentialist thought opposes itself to tidy systems and overzealous trust in rationality. When Charlie Brown comes to Dr. Lucy van Pelt in 1973 believing that his trouble in life is moral uncertainty, she reassures him and sends him off, but two panels later he's already back at the psychiatric booth: "I was wrong . . . It didn't help . . . You need more in life than just having someone around to tell you when you're doing the right thing . . ."

No textbook, no matter how advanced, could ever adequately describe, let alone prescribe, the experience of being human—of living and acting in the present moment. Naturally, existential philosophers disagree with one another about human experience, too. What unites them as existentialists is that this part of us, the part that escapes comprehensive description or rule-binding, is the most important part: as we act, we choose what to become, and what we become establishes our identities. So meaning is what we make of *ourselves*.

There are certain facts about each of us: a face, an age, an ethnicity, abilities, memories, relationships, desires, and the like. Some of the facts we can change; some we can't. But in terms of who we're becoming, none of those facts can be separated from how we see ourselves—how we relate to and interpret them. So even though I can't choose to be literally anything—as Charlie Brown has it when he complains to

Snoopy, "Why aren't you two ponies?"—there are still infinitely many ways to be myself (or a suburban beagle).

And in the words of German existentialist Martin Heidegger (1889–1976), existence is "care"; no matter how we feel about ourselves, insofar as we exist as humans, we can't help but *matter* to ourselves. Even wanting to die or feeling ambivalent about death is a stance toward oneself. In some ways our existence is "for itself"—happening to itself, happening for its own sake—and those ways are hidden from other people and separate from the dimension of our existence directed at them. So no one else's systems, based on external descriptions, can fully sum us up or tell us what to do.

Existentialism suggests its own standard for how to live: authenticity. Being authentic means recognizing that I can take responsibility for who I am, actively accepting that responsibility, and committing every aspect of myself in an ongoing way to my undertakings or "projects." This isn't the same as striving to be the "master of my fate"; authenticity isn't about whether my projects succeed, or even about what they are. It's about how thoroughly I employ my whole self toward them.

Authenticity isn't about factual truth—how things look from an external perspective—but about remaining faithful or "true" to what you are. We can learn here from Peppermint Patty, who turns overzealous while taking a True or False exam: "Everything is true! Nothing is false! The whole world is true! We're all true!" She's right that the world is "true" in that it's being itself and "doing its thing"; Heidegger says the world is always "world-ing." But her last statement needs adjustment: unlike insentient beings, people must root out their self-deceptions, discover and accept themselves, and "live their truth" in order to be "true" in the highest sense available to them.

In contrast, living inauthentically means passively inhabiting the roles, attitudes, beliefs, and projects proposed to you by your surroundings. It's to be anonymous even to yourself, existing without awareness of your existence and of the possibility of choosing it freely and responsibly.

3eanuts: Providing Your Fill of the Void, Three Squares a Day

To arrive at authenticity, we first need to experience the realities that underlie our responsibility for shaping ourselves. *Peanuts* excels at depicting and highlighting the kinds of moments that often accompany such experiences. In existentialism, these experiences get labels like "the absurd," "anxiety," and "despair."

Charles Schulz fought in World War II in Europe as these ideas were becoming popular there, and his first comic strip *Li'l Folks*, a sort of one-panel proto-*Peanuts*, hit newspapers less than two years after the war's end. *Peanuts* often covers up these moments, though, as soon as they happen—just like life does. The typical formula runs like this: In the first three (or however many) panels, a situation plays out which might shake the characters—and readers—out of inauthentic ways of existing. Then in the final panel, a joke or gag breaks the tension, permitting the moment to pass without being directly faced and addressed in all its implications. This is where *3eanuts* comes in.

In 2011, I was on vacation at the beach with my best friend Max, waiting out the rain in a bookstore. I showed him some of the more gut-wrenching comics in the *Peanuts* collection I'd been browsing, and soon we realized we could heighten the effect in most of these by covering up and ignoring the last panel. A few weeks later, inspired by bleak comic remixes like *Garfield Minus Garfield* and *Nietzsche Family Circus*, I made a website for the most dismal tailless strips. Since weekday *Peanuts* until the late Eighties were usually four panels long, the shortened versions became "3eanuts."

The site went live on March 25th 2011 and went viral within a few days, getting over a million hits and garnering write-ups online from *Time, Entertainment Weekly*, and the *Washington Post*. Much of this attention could be chalked up to nostalgia—the site gives an excuse to revisit a childhood favorite—plus nihilism—the anarchic pleasure of seeing something often considered innocent and sentimental, even to the point of kitsch (think inspirational *Peanuts* posters in elementary schools, Snoopy greeting cards for every occasion, and the like), twisted to serve a bleakly ironic postmodern sensibility. But even so, something about these stripped-down cartoons hit home.

The Groundlessness of Grounders

One might wonder: What's the value of leaving things open-ended? Well, that's just it—it exposes the open-endedness or "groundlessness" of value itself. In other words, I don't know of any timeless, unchanging, universally important ground to build on. Once I realize that the only ground I have is my finite, mortal self and the world I'm in, I can get started building in the appropriate way.

Lucy explains this perfectly to Charlie Brown in 1963, overlooking the horizon in another hillside epiphany: "As far as you know, this is the only world there is . . . Right? There are no other worlds for you to live in . . . Right? You were born to live in this world . . . Right? WELL, LIVE IN IT, THEN!"

This kind of mountaintop realization tends to elude us in everyday life at sea level. When life is going as expected and I'm absorbed in my activities, the universe actually seems to serve them. What I notice around me fits conveniently into the story I'm telling myself about myself. But I don't notice my noticing. That is, I don't see how I'm noticing selectively to make things fit while I'm doing it—things just seem to hum along as they should. It's only if something disturbs the positive connection between my purposes and the world, breaking down that imaginary "should," that I can "snap out of it" and notice the connection itself.

When the universe suddenly seems to be "out of tune" with my purposes, I may experience "the absurd" (literally, "the out-of-tune"). To experience the absurd is to notice that, however I suppose this connection to be, the connection isn't inherent in reality itself; I impose it on my experience artificially. So once I've experienced out-of-tuneness, I can see that the sense of humming-along is just as much a ground for meaning as the sense of out-of-tuneness. An even more profound disharmony is that, since my own mode of existence toward myself is "care," I deeply want existence itself to "care" about me—but it doesn't, at least not in the way I want. To go on living knowing I can't live without wanting this, yet it isn't and won't be the case: this is to live a contradiction—an absurd one.

For instance, in a strip from 1967, after Charlie Brown has lost yet another ballgame, he stays on the pitcher's mound and bemoans the meaninglessness not merely of the loss, but of the game itself: "I think that's what bothers me most . . . We get beaten, and no one even knows about it . . . Our games aren't even important . . ." Because of a disappointment, he realizes that even if he'd won, achieving the traditional goal of physical and tactical prowess in America's pastime would only give him a fleeting thrill; it wouldn't give his life meaning.

True, he does still hold out hope that a larger audience would make the game "important," but this is evidence that he's reaching the cusp of the absurd—he's acknowledging that his hopes are misplaced, yet refusing to let go of them.

On this occasion, the fourth panel deflates not by diverting from the moment or trivializing it, but by inflating it to the popping point. In that panel, Charlie Brown walks away saying, with a tinge of ironic melodrama, "I think I'll go home, and lie in a dark room . . ." Removing the last panel denies us the satisfaction of seeing the ever-heightened suffering through to its logical conclusion—the situation's last vestige of an underlying sense of order and control.

Punchlines relieve tension, and for the existentialist, it's crucial to linger in the tension long and often enough to let go of our coping mechanisms and accept reality the way it is. As Lucy puts it to Charlie in 1957, "What this world needs is more troubled minds! A TROUBLED MIND IN A TROUBLED WORLD!!!" This strip, incidentally, uses the same popping-point tactic in the final panel: "A TROUBLED WORLD IN A TROUBLED UNIVERSE . . . A . . ." Charlie: "Good grief!" Yes, to misquote Gordon Gekko, "Grief is good."

Young Goodman Brown

The "fine day" hasn't come yet—in Charlie's life or in ours. If we keep basing our hopes and values on it, we'll keep being disappointed, day in and day out. Even if we do keep hoping for removal from groundlessness, alienation, and the rest, there's a silver lining—for most of us.

Life usually has ups and downs, so we get at least some satisfaction. But for Charlie, the downs are so interminable that hope makes no sense; he will always lose to the kite-eating tree, the empty mailbox, and the other team. The exceptions to this in *Peanuts* prove the rule: for instance, when Charlie's team actually does win a game—its first—in 1958, it's when Charlie's on sick leave. They win not despite their manager's absence, but because of it: "We didn't do anything you told us! In fact, we didn't even miss you!" What's more, Charlie's illness was brought on by his anxiousness about the team's performance; reviewing stats from practice the day before the game, he moans, "Suddenly my stomach hurts, and I feel all alone . . ."

Nausea, angst, dread—all of these feelings are alienating: they happen to *you*, and they serve as a boundary from others insofar as the feelings can't be fully revealed or shared. Yet they also make the boundary between self and world fuzzier. No matter how much you might want to escape them, you can't stop feeling what you feel, even though it arrives uninvited from someplace other than the self.

Charlie suffers from not being able to be what he feels a need to be—a good baseball manager—and this affliction is uniquely his own. But if he feels he's alone and "not like himself," that also means he hasn't fully lost the underlying "he"—the one who's really in there, feeling this. This is how Heidegger turns Descartes' "thinking thing" (the "I" of "I think, therefore I am") into the existential Dasein, or "Being-there"; if I'm raising the question of what it means to be, then there must be a type of being for whom its own way of be-ing is an issue. No matter how deeply I sink into despair, there's still an inner place where it's happening, so all is not lost.

This still seems like cold comfort at best. So what's there to gain when things always end up going downhill? Albert Camus (1913–1960) wrote about the mythical character Sisyphus in terms that suit Schulz's bleak landscapes. In the myth, Sisyphus is condemned to spend eternity rolling a massive boulder up a mountain, only to have the boulder slip from his hands just before reaching the summit and roll back to the bottom every time.

As Sisyphus descends to start anew, Camus imagines that he does so not by anyone else's prodding, but by his own choice—not out of passive obedience to his fate, but out of revolt against it. He accepts that he cannot have the external reality or the fate he'd like, but he refuses to let it define him, vowing instead to cultivate an authentic inner life. He asserts himself through the only means available to him: saying *yes* to his task.

Sisyphus rolls the boulder each time with every intention of reaching the top, and when it rolls back down, he regroups and starts over, because he believes that, in a good world, he'd be allowed to succeed. It's a form of protest through hyper-obedience. Yet at the same time, he is learning to say, "All is well." As Camus writes, "The struggle itself toward the heights is enough to fill a man's heart. One must imagine Sisyphus happy."

I Got a Rock

Sisyphus is the everyman—just replace "pushing a boulder" with "coping with finitude." And for millions of people the world over, for sixty-five years and counting, so is Charlie. There aren't many American names more generic than "Charlie Brown." In fact, the name Charles comes from a word for "man." And brown is a mix of all colors; the word's

Old English precursor simply meant any dark shade.

It's worth noting, too, that "Schulz" comes from a word for a law enforcement officer or mayor or judge: someone who's a professional advocate of rigid human ethical systems. Suppose such a person were "condemned" to draw inside the lines of boxes, day after month after year. Imagine if this person were to rebel against limits—by filling each day's ordained boxes, for longer than anyone else ever has, with superficially saccharine but subtly subversive cartoons, parables of despair . . .

One fine day, Lucy holds a football. She persuades Charlie to come running up and kick it. He tries with all his might. He has failed many times; it makes him tired, frustrated, and skeptical, but it doesn't make him stop. He kicks at nothing, spinning, groundless, disoriented.

He does it because he can't help but believe in a world without boxes, beyond them, one where nothing is pulled out from under you; a world that isn't a joke at your expense; a world without end. It may not exist anywhere else, but in that moment, it exists in Charlie Brown.

3
Can Charlie Brown Be Happy?

JENNIFER BAKER

Charlie Brown often complains that he's not happy. At first glance, there seems to be an obvious reason for this—he's a loser. But things aren't quite so simple.

According to ancient thinkers such as Plato, Aristotle, the Stoics, and the Epicureans, there's a connection between being happy and being a good person. To be truly happy, you have to have managed something internal and philosophical.

Winning isn't enough, you must be ethical too. Otherwise, if you're a winner, the world will love you, but you won't even like yourself, at least not properly.

We call these ancient philosophers virtue ethicists, and of all ethical theorists, it's the virtue ethicists who do the best job of worrying about the winners. The *winners*, you say? Who needs to worry about them? Can't they look after themselves?

The ancient Greek ethicists give us two reasons why we should indeed worry about the winners. Winners accumulate great power, so the damage they might do is significant. And also, winners are easily distracted from what makes for true happiness. They may have been told that becoming a movie star, or wealthy, or an Olympian would make them content. But it doesn't. Contentment actually requires something else.

Winners find a lot to recommend in the ancient approach. Ryan Holiday's pithy restatement of Stoicism, *The Obstacle Is the Way*, is not only a fabulous best-seller, but, as Greg Bishop reports, has become the bible of such high-performance stars as Arnold Schwarzenegger, Irish tennis pro James McGee, NFL lineman Garrett Gilkey, and Olympian cross-country skier Chandra Crawford, among many, many others.

But how does the Stoic game plan apply to well-meaning, level-headed, conscientious losers of the Charlie Brown type? What advice could Marcus Aurelius or Ryan Holiday offer Charlie Brown? Or a Cubs fan (unless this is really their year)?

Other People as a Challenge to Happiness

Other people are one problem for Charlie Brown. Schulz sets this up in the very first *Peanuts* strip. Two children watch Charlie Brown pass by, calling him "Good ol' Charlie Brown." Once he passes, though, a child goes, "How I hate him." The theme of our complex feelings for others is on display, and Schulz has us hooked.

Philosophers have often suggested that we're less loved by others than we might think, and psychologists have found the same thing: research reported by Karen Riddel shows that only about fifty percent of those you think of as your friends think of you as their friend! But Schulz, though he strikes some existentialist notes here and there, is not pushing the grim theory that we're all alien to each other and to ourselves.

It is not generalized pessimism on which Schulz alights: it's our particular reaction to Charlie Brown, a well-meaning shy kid (a kindergartener if we're to believe there could be a bunch of kindergarteners quite as articulate as these). Some of the *Peanuts* characters, like Linus and Schroeder, are comparatively at ease with themselves. Others have social burdens very unlike Charlie's—Peppermint Patty is not shy. The particular "problem" of being Charlie is one the other kids call out by name. His name.

VIOLET: Sometimes I get so mad at you . . . you . . . you . . . you . . . you ol' Charlie Brown!!!

CHARLIE BROWN: [*sincerely hurt*] What an insult!

Even sweet Linus experiences it:

Charlie Brown, you're the only person I know who can take a wonderful season like Christmas and turn it into a problem. Maybe Lucy's right. Of all the Charlie Browns in the world, you're the Charlie Browniest.

What is it that makes us so impatient and cruel to the shy? Perhaps the answer has to wait on us figuring out shyness itself, and psychologists still do not agree upon a single account. They do seem to agree that it is not the same as introversion and only partly neuroticism, and Susan Cain has made a strong case for the vital role of introverts. On the other hand, who's unfamiliar with the feeling? Shy people get annoyed with other shy people. As readers we have sympathy galore for a humble, misunderstood, cautious protagonist. But put us behind a person struggling awkwardly to get out her words, and we feel as impatient and as imperious as Lucy Van Pelt

Giving up Home Runs

If Schulz hadn't used a sports field as the setting for the *Peanuts* gang so often, he would have told us much less. Our traditional sports ethos says that playing sports will strengthen your character. It's something about the discipline of taking the losses and continuing to play. Charlie Brown ought to be a candidate then, for a sports-strengthened character.

Again and again we see Charlie Brown playing (kicking, pitching, managing the team) to the best of his ability. And yet, when does the transformation happen? Schulz never lets us see Charlie Brown being anything but dejected by his losses on the field. Yes, he's rule-following, devoted, and sincere, but is this enough? A second challenge to anyone with an account of happiness: in order to be happy, do we also need to have the wins?

Feeling Unhappy

Lucy: Snap out of it. Five cents please.

Charlie Brown says to Linus: "I think there must be something wrong with me, Linus, Christmas is coming, but I am not happy. I don't feel the way I am supposed to feel." It may seem to go without saying that a person experiencing depression is not happy. A person (and child) who is depressed will not feel happy, but it is also not right to assume such a person will not be happy if we only consider a longer span of time.

Haybron on Happiness

In *The Pursuit of Unhappiness: The Elusive Psychology of Well-Being*, Daniel Haybron argues that happiness is not just *one* thing. It's not pleasure, not memories, not how well-off we are. It cannot even be how happy we report that we are. When asked about our level of happiness, too much depends on whose happiness we're comparing ours to at that moment or what our expectations are.

Happiness, Haybron argues, is best regarded as an emotional condition. We talk of *episodes* of depression. Happiness is like an episode, Haybron maintains. It lasts about that long, and it should not be assessed over a lifetime nor an afternoon. He explains that we can represent happiness only if we acknowledge that it has three dimensions. We experience different amounts of happiness along each dimension. Haybron's three dimensions are *being attuned*, *being engaged*, and *experiencing endorsement*.

- **Attunement** is peace of mind and a lack of anxiety. It's confidence and a lack of insecurity. Haybron has described it as an ability to roll with the punches. Charlie Brown does not do that well. He is not wholly unconfident, either, but he is nervous and self-conscious. I think he'd agree that he is not fully "attuned."

As Charlie Brown says, "Sometimes you lie in bed at night, and you don't have a single thing to worry about . . . That always worries me!" "Be a Linus, not a Charlie Brown" is advice I've been given before. Linus, self-aware and reflective, is capable of weathering all sorts of disappointments with philosophical calm. That kid is pretty attuned.

- **Engagement** includes exuberance and vitality. It's not being listless. Haybron includes experiences of "flow" in "engagement." Boredom is counted out. Charlie Brown seems rather happy along this dimension. He gets plenty excited at wins, he tries at many, many things. He does not have the type of social anxiety that keeps a person at home, and he is, if anything, a doer.

- **Endorsement** is a matter of feeling joy rather than sadness. It is being cheerful rather than irritable. Charlie Brown so often reports feeling bad. He knows it is not normal, and he asks for help. He owns his attitudes.

Haybron believes that Americans are very focused on endorsement, often at the expense of being able to fully capture the rest of what we mean by happiness. Charlie Brown's shyness is repellent to others. Might it be that a person who fails to endorse the activities they are participating in with others causes those others quite a bit of anxiety? If the others need to endorse what they are doing to be happy, being made unsure about the value of the activity puts something important at risk.

If one kid is not excited about going on vacation, might it mean that we have all been fooled by what we are supposed to find fun? Imagine our worries about that kind of thing catching on. Every time Charlie Brown is accused of bringing the others down, I think this is the explanation as to why. He's clearly a thinker, he is clearly an active participant, and he has not ended up with the same endorsement as the others.

Haybron would not think that Charlie Brown's lack of happiness is some kind of failing or that Charlie Brown should simply do things differently in order to be happy. He's already social and active and engaged in meaningful projects.

Charlie Brown lacks endorsement and attunement. And he may forever be unable to feel as unworried or cheerful as others, given what may already be fixed in his personality.

Charlie Brown as Hero

Why do so many of us see Charlie Brown as a sort of hero? Most readers of *Peanuts* not only sympathize with Charlie Brown, they *admire* him. We do! Wouldn't his peers be surprised? Christopher Caldwell has written beautifully about this in his essay "Against Snoopy":

> What makes Charlie Brown such a rich character is that he's not purely a loser. The self-loathing that causes him so much anguish is decidedly *not* self-effacement. Charlie Brown is optimistic enough to think he can *earn* a sense of self-worth, and his willingness to do so by exposing himself to humiliations is the dramatic engine that drives the strip. The greatest of Charlie Brown's virtues is his resilience, which is to say his courage. Charlie Brown is ambitious. He *manages* the baseball team. He's the pitcher, not a scrub. He may be a loser, but he's, strangely, a leader at the same time. This makes his mood swings truly bipolar in their magnificence: he vacillates not between kinda happy and kinda unhappy, but between being a 'hero' and being a 'goat'. ("Against Snoopy")

As a virtue ethicist, I'm always pleased to see compliments put in such terms. Turning to the ancients will explain how a loser can also be a leader; what Charlie Brown might be aiming for in his relentless attempts to improve; and why his moods vacillate so much. His moods vacillate, the ancients would tell him, because he is in dire need of their philosophy on life.

Ancient Happiness

LINUS: Well, I can understand how you feel. You worked hard, studying for the spelling bee, and I suppose you feel you let everyone down, and you made a fool of yourself and everything. But did you notice something, Charlie Brown?

CHARLIE BROWN: What's that?

LINUS: The world didn't come to an end.

Aristotle explains that ultimately, what we are *all* aiming for is happiness. This is the "eudaemonist axiom" stated by Gregory Vlastos as: "Happiness is desired by all human beings as the ultimate end of all their rational acts." So Aristotle does not conceive of happiness in terms of a mood, and certainly not as pure preference-satisfaction or pleasure-seeking. Happiness is no warm puppy.

Instead, Aristotle suggests we must transform ourselves, developing a second nature, so that we can experience what our psychological design lends itself to: a kind of ethical integrity that makes choosing good behavior a joy. Julia Annas describes the result of developing virtue as a kind of flow experience.

> Flow results when a person whose goals are harmoniously integrated engages in activity in which intelligent and focused attention is brought to bear on goal-directed activity in such a way that the activity is found intrinsically rewarding. (*Intelligent Virtue*, p. 72)

The traditional virtue ethicists are recommending something very distinctive: the goals the agent is to have can only be ethical goals. Happiness cannot come from pursuing a goal such as "I will be drafted by the NBA." It requires that we aim for something like "I will always think of what others feel like when one side wins."

Charlie Brown pursues and endorses personal norms just like this one. As Christopher Caldwell writes, "When Linus gives him a gripping recap of a football game in which a team facing a six-point deficit scored a spectacular touchdown with three seconds left, Charlie Brown asks only, 'How did the other team feel?' He is a deeply good person." So why isn't he, on the ancient account, happy?

My actual answer has to do with what it takes to be a good person (no child can manage it!). But let me consider another response first. We could certainly worry whether the ancient accounts of virtue did not recognize the role of personality or depression. But if you look to Aristotle's student's work or to the Stoics, you find that they see personalities as crucial to how we function in the world, but not crucial to our ethics. They talk about how personality is like a mask we wear that is permanently affixed.

A Charlie Brown will never become a reckless heartbreaker; his dour personality is more like a given. Is he then ruled out as a candidate for happiness, due to something like personality, which can easily be seen as beyond his control?

For the Stoics, the answer's clearly no. The well-intentioned Charlie Brown is not prevented from being ethical, as phlegmatic as he is. True, he has not been blessed with what Aristotle calls "natural virtue." Such a person just never gets tempted to darker motivations because people, naturally, react kindly to what must be a sunny and open personality. But "natural virtue" is not true virtue, and it falls apart when put to severe tests. True virtue (and so happiness) comes out of the hard work and struggle and self-control it takes to become a good person, one who really identifies with and enjoys the good things he does. Charlie Brown is not "a good person" yet (a mere child!). But he is primed to train himself to become a virtuous person.

We see some of that at work in the *Peanuts* strips. What a child is getting from his upbringing, with all the coaxing, and reminding, and role modeling that we do, includes practice in identifying with and following norms which we regard as ethical. These are always contextual, always a matter of our culture (though the standards invoked can be recognized outside of it) and we probably borrow these from our peers as much as from our parents. But wherever they might come from, to follow good norms properly is, for virtue ethics, a matter of self-identification with them.

You do this, on the ancient account, not by trying to be like other people but by trying to find the right norms and then being motivated by them. Norms concern a generalized, typically third-person, description of some specified behavior. Aristotle discusses how to repay debts, and writes: "To all older persons, too, one should give honor appropriate to their age, by rising to receive them and finding seats for them and so on." Later virtue ethicists present their audience with norms like "Do not show off with a gold wine goblet when silver will do," "Do not get carried away by crowds," and "Educate your daughters like your sons." Schulz provides quite a few modern norms directly to us.

Both tasks—identifying the right norms, then being motivated by them—take a lot of work and a lot of self-control. To do the sorting work, you also need to have the right philosophy about life. This is where the ancients would say Charlie Brown's problem lies.

Virtue Ethics on Losing and Feeling Bad

"I used to say that he tried too hard," Charles Schulz remembers about his early treatment of Charlie, "and that he wanted everyone to like him too much, but I've grown away from that" (quoted in "Against Snoopy"). The ancients would track Charlie Brown's unhappiness to his dependence on the approval of others. The ancient virtue ethicists would really encourage Charlie Brown to recognize others' approval for what it is: the approval of the confused.

The Stoics would be a wonderful guide to how you can find strength in disapproval. It just becomes a challenge, another way to steel yourself to do the right thing. The "naturally virtuous" do not have true virtue; they just have an easy time. The Stoics would find Charlie Brown's shyness to be material for virtue. That negative leads to a positive, if being virtuous is the goal.

The Stoics would also recommend that Charlie Brown should change his view of winning. Yes, he admires a bench warmer, and yes, he's sincere and dedicated, but the Stoics would need him to be even more confident that winning is not the point of playing a game. The point of playing is to exhibit good character—a loss is nothing to such a person focused on virtue.

Cicero puts it this way: "We do not think that virtue is like navigation or medicine. Rather it is like . . . acting or dancing . . . Here the end, namely the performance of the skill, is contained within the skill itself, not sought outside it." You lose no virtue through losing (though you might lose it through winning!) *How* you play the game is everything, no matter how high the stakes seem.

> According to Epictetus, Socrates [at his trial] was like a man playing ball. And at that time and place, what was the ball that he was playing with? Imprisonment, exile, drinking poison, being deprived of wife, leaving children orphans. These were the things with which he was playing, but nonetheless he played and handled the ball in good form. So ought we also to act, exhibiting the ball-player's carefulness about the game but the same indifference about the outcome. (*The Morality of Happiness*, p. 402)

In fact, all of life is like a game, the ancients tell us. The philosophers William Stephens and Randolph Feezell explain further. They connect the habits of sports players to the Stoic recommendation that we always keep in mind what we cannot control:

> When faced with a challenge that tests our ability to endure, to persevere, and to overcome, the Stoic embraces the opportunity to exercise his virtuous traits of character. By responding to a trying situation with patience, one strengthens one's ability to be patient in the future. By dealing with turmoil with poise, one strengthens one's ability to be calm in the future. By refusing to be provoked by someone who is abusive or insulting, one frees oneself from the destructiveness of anger. ("The Ideal of the Stoic Sportsman")

Ancient virtue ethics would like to see a good man recognize some things the child Charlie Brown does not.

The way others treat him does not truly matter, and can be a source of strength.

The wins do not truly matter.

What he can do and control matters, and what he can do and control is being ethical.

He is not an ace pitcher, or the coolest guy in the class, but he can still be all that he needs to be.

Maybe, once this message is received, we can imagine Charlie Brown happy.

II

Good Ol' Metaphysics

4
Is It God or the Great Pumpkin, Charlie Brown?

Jamie Carlin Watson

Let's face it, it's weird to believe in the Great Pumpkin—a mysterious being who rises each Halloween from the most sincere pumpkin patch to hand out toys to children. But in *It's the Great Pumpkin, Charlie Brown* (1966), Linus is devoted to the idea, and for no apparent reason.

Could this belief be rational? Is it ever rational to believe in something like the Great Pumpkin? And, more interestingly, is belief in the Great Pumpkin like belief in God?

Some philosophers argue that belief in God is dangerously similar to sitting up all night waiting for the Great Pumpkin; they say it's irrational to believe anything without sufficient evidence. And like the Great Pumpkin, there isn't enough evidence for God. Others argue that belief in God can be rational even if we have no evidence for it, though not belief in the Great Pumpkin. How could this be?

It's the Great Pumpkin, Charlie Brown raises interesting questions about what makes a belief rational. As we will see, evidence isn't all there is to having rational beliefs. And on at least one view of what makes a belief worth having, even some Pumpkin-style beliefs are rational.

But this doesn't mean that anything goes, that people can rationally believe whatever they want. In fact, Linus believes in the Great Pumpkin even when this belief conflicts with what makes beliefs worth having. This suggests that his belief in the Great Pumpkin is irrational. But does it imply the same about belief in God?

What's So Weird about Believing in the Great Pumpkin?

People believe weird things all the time. Some people are convinced that Rhonda Byrne's *The Secret* (2006) holds key insights into the universe. Other people believe in ghosts and trust astrological predictions while living otherwise non-weird lives. Is Linus's belief in the Great Pumpkin like these other weird beliefs? And is a weird belief necessarily irrational?

One thing that sets Linus's belief apart from other weird beliefs is that he's the only person who believes it. Enthusiasts of *The Secret* have a social network, albeit small, as do fans of the paranormal and the zodiac. People often use the experiences and beliefs of others to help confirm or disconfirm their own beliefs, even if they don't always arrive at the most rational conclusions. But none of Linus's friends believes in the Great Pumpkin. Not even Sally, who's willing to play along so she can spend time with him. We in the audience are a bit baffled, too. We never learn where this story comes from or whether anyone else in the *Peanuts* universe accepts it. We have no reason to think the Great Pumpkin has ever shown up with toys for anyone anywhere.

Despite this, we might not judge Linus too harshly. The Great Pumpkin is similar to other childhood myths, like the Easter Bunny and Santa Claus, which are also elusive magical beings who bring gifts to children who are "good." And perhaps there is something valuable about the childhood belief in magic, such as increased creativity and an aspiration for a moral ideal.

But children of a certain age often have quite good reasons to believe the classic myths. They are accompanied by tangible experiences: eggs or toys on Eastertide, presents on Christmas morning. And children's social world largely corroborates these stories. For example, parents, extended family members, television commercials, holiday movies, and shopping malls all suggest that Santa is real, and charitable, and responsible for the gifts on Christmas morning. But there is no tangible experience associated with the Great Pumpkin and no corroboration for it. So, belief in the Great Pumpkin is different from classic childhood myths in really important ways.

Even still, there might be other good reasons for thinking Linus's belief is not so weird as to be irrational. For instance, we might think of Linus's commitment to the Great Pumpkin as mere make-believe, such as having an imaginary friend or Snoopy's recurring fantasy of being a World War I flying ace. There is no tangible experience associated with such beliefs, and they are not widely corroborated by anyone (apart from parents or friends who play along). Yet, there is something endearing about Snoopy's gallant battles and harrowing escapes from danger behind enemy lines. Through make-believe, children can learn to value justice, emulate heroic behavior, and form healthy self-narratives. If belief in the Great Pumpkin were like this, it might not be so bad.

But notice that Snoopy never confuses his fantasy world with the real world. Sometimes he obstinately persists in the fantasy, but we never think he can't tell the difference between the fantasy and reality. This means that Snoopy doesn't actually *believe* he is a World War I flying ace. Not believing in fantasies seems essential for make-believe to be rational. And unlike Snoopy, Linus *does* believe the Great Pumpkin exists. He not only writes the Great Pumpkin a letter, he adds the postscript: "If you really are a fake, don't tell me. I don't wanna know."

He intentionally tries to insulate himself against evidence that would threaten his belief. Even his attempt to insulate himself is incoherent, since if the Great Pumpkin doesn't exist, it would not exist to respect his request not to tell him. Here we learn that believing the Great Pumpkin exists is more important to him than whether the belief is actually true.

In short, what makes Linus's belief in the Great Pumpkin *so* weird is that it is not based on any *evidence*: his friends do not believe it, there is no tangible experience of it, and it is not corroborated by his wider culture. Further, he tries to avoid evidence that it isn't true.

Traditionally, philosophers have called beliefs that are unsupported by evidence *irrational*. For a belief to be rational, so the view goes, we must have good evidence for it, and that evidence must outweigh any reasons we might have for not believing it. Also, we must be at least somewhat open to the possibility that we are wrong, keeping an eye out for reasons that would challenge the belief. This helps us discard beliefs when we discover new evidence against them, it helps us avoid beliefs that aren't likely to be true, and it helps us to decide just how strongly we should believe something.

For some children, it might be rational to believe in Santa Claus for a while because their experiences suggest it is true. But as they grow up, their confidence should wane; they will have experiences that suggest their original reasons for believing are too weak. (*He does all that in one night? He visits every child in the world?*) But this classic view of evidence faces some pretty tough problems. And to know whether Linus's belief is really irrational, we need to know whether these problems can be overcome.

The Classic View of Evidence

Most of the kids in *Peanuts* are like us when it comes to belief: we want all of our beliefs to be true. Frustrated with Linus, Charlie Brown asks, "When are you going to stop believing in something that isn't true?" Offended, Linus fires back with skepticism about "that fellow in the red suit with the white beard who goes, 'Ho, ho, ho.'"

This reminds us that reality is messy, and we often believe false things. Ptolemy had good reasons to believe the Earth is at the center of the universe, but he was wrong. Isaac Newton had good reasons for believing space and time are two, distinct things, though we now believe he was mistaken. Charlie Brown is perhaps a bit unsure of his reasons for believing in Santa Claus, so he isn't interested in comparing evidence. Instead, he chalks up his disagreement with Linus to "denominational differences."

"Denomination" is a term commonly used to distinguish different doctrines among Christian Protestants. For example, Presbyterian, Methodist, and Church of God are different denominations of Protestantism. While some Protestants call Catholicism and Orthodoxy denominations, few Catholics or Orthodox use the term.

Most of us like to think we hold our beliefs on the basis of evidence. We think that supporting evidence is a *good reason to believe a claim is true.* There are lots of bad reasons to believe something is true, such as Sally's believing Linus about the Great Pumpkin because she is attracted to Linus (a phenomenon called *beauty bias*) and Charlie Brown's believing Lucy won't pull the football away because she gave him a signed contract saying she wouldn't.

But we get along better in the world when we believe for good reasons. For instance, when crossing the street, looking both ways has proved more successful than simply *wishing* or *guessing*. And we often trust our doctors over our (non-physician) friends to tell us whether the feelings of illness we are experiencing are caused by, say, strep throat or the flu. Doctors tend to be a better source of evidence for such questions than, say, our friends and families.

These examples suggest a popular view of rationality: a person is rational only if her beliefs are based on evidence and that evidence isn't outweighed by any other evidence to the contrary. Now, the fact that evidence can be weighed (metaphorically, of course) suggests that rational support comes in degrees. The more rocks Charlie Brown gets for tricks-or-treats, the stronger his belief should be that he won't get any candy.

The strongest evidence is often the most *basic.* Basic beliefs need no other beliefs for support. For example, sense experience (like seeing a pile of leaves and smelling pumpkin-flavored lattes) and claims that seem obviously true (such as "2 + 2 = 4" and "No bachelors are married") tend to support other beliefs without needing their own support.

On the classic view, beliefs are rational if they are *basic* or they *follow logically from basic beliefs* (for instance, "If no bachelors are married and Linus is a bachelor, then we may believe *Linus is not married*").

This sounds like a pretty good theory. And well-respected philosophers like John Locke and David Hume held views very similar to this. Unfortunately, if it's right, most of our beliefs are irrational. Consider *memories*. They are not obviously true (we've all misremembered things). They are not a kind of sense experience (though our senses were used to form most of them). And they do not follow logically from either obviously true claims or sense experience. The philosopher Alvin Plantinga gives the following example:

> You ask me what I had for breakfast; I think for a moment and then remember: pancakes and blueberries. I don't argue from the fact that it seems to me that I remember having pancakes for breakfast to the conclusion I did; rather, you ask me what I had for breakfast, and the answer simply comes to mind. (*Warranted Christian Belief*, pp. 175–76)

According to the traditional view of evidence, this belief is irrational. But that seems strange. Most of our beliefs are formed this way: Our parents tell us something and we just believe it. We have beliefs about how to get to work, that going trick-or-treating is legal, the names of our relatives, even our birthdays, all without the slightest thought of what evidence we have for them or how strong that evidence is. If the classic theory of evidence is right, then most of our beliefs are irrational most of the time.

Further, the truth of some beliefs actually depends on whether we believe them. If I am running a foot race and the competition looks much fitter than I am, I have two options. I can believe strictly according to the evidence, and conclude that I will not likely win. Or, I can be a little overconfident and believe I will win despite the evidence. In these cases, a little overconfidence can actually increase the likelihood that the belief will be true.

Further still, some beliefs are valuable even when they are not true. Consider an example from the medical field, where hoping against the evidence is sometimes encouraged. In 2002, researchers found that aging patients who had hopeful attitudes ended up having better lung function, across a ten-year period, than patients who had pessimistic attitudes (Kubzansky, "Breathing Easy").

Other studies show that people who are more optimistic tend to suffer less and live longer than people who are unwilling to hope beyond the evidence (Maruta in the *Mayo Clinic Proceedings*). This suggests that some beliefs are worth having even if they are not based on good evidence.

And finally, the most damaging critique of all is that the very belief "You should believe only what is obvious or what can be derived from what is obvious" fails its own test. It is not obviously true and it doesn't follows from beliefs that are.

Given that all these beliefs seem perfectly reasonable despite what the classic view says, and given that the classic view fails its own test, we have good reasons to look elsewhere for what makes a belief rational. But is there a good alternative to the classic view that makes sense? Should we just resign ourselves to the possibility that most of our beliefs are irrational?

Rationality as Virtue

One alternative is to say that it is just *not practical* to doubt most of our beliefs, even if they aren't rational. First, we don't have time to gather evidence for every belief (there wouldn't be time for Halloween parties or trick-or-treating). And second, there are many beliefs for which we may never have sufficient evidence (are you *certain* that you're a "good person" or that you won't get into a car wreck on the way to work?).

While this option explains why it's *useful* to believe these things, it doesn't explain why it's *good* to believe them in a knowledge-seeking sense (which is called the *epistemic* sense from the Greek word for knowledge: *episteme*). A better response is that what makes them rational is that the beliefs are formed *well*, that is, *responsibly*.

We form beliefs responsibly when we consider, in addition to evidence, what makes a belief worth having. For instance, a belief is worth having if it is likely to be true. A belief is also valuable if it helps make sense of our relationships and the world around us. Few of us question whether our parents love us with the critical analysis that philosophers suggest. We accept that they love us because doing so fosters the relationship better than challenging every expression of love. Sally's reaction to Linus can help us with this view.

When Sally first shows up to the pumpkin patch, she is skeptical. She has admitted to Lucy that there *might* be a Great Pumpkin, but she's concerned that the others are right and that Linus is making a fool of himself. Linus is surprised at her skepticism, expecting her to be "innocent and trusting." But Sally proves shrewder than that. In the end, she decides she should stay and wait for more evidence (mostly because she has a crush on Linus). Is her belief that she should do this rational?

Clearly, evidence is important. If Sally thought Linus were prone to hallucinations or that he regularly lies, then it would be irresponsible for her to believe he might be right about the Great Pumpkin. But in this case, her evidence is inconclusive, so she is in a predicament: she can hang around and wait for more evidence, or she can join her friends for tricks-or-treats. While she wants to know whether the Great Pumpkin exists, the value of knowing that is in conflict with the value of tricks-or-treats. Notice that evidence cannot help her decide between those two. She has to decide whether it's *worth it to her* to wait for evidence of the Great Pumpkin. This means that a belief's rationality depends partly on the belief's *value* to her.

Further, Sally has to decide how *likely* it is that waiting in the pumpkin patch will tell her accurately whether the Great Pumpkin exists. Apparently, whether the Great Pumpkin shows up depends on whether Linus's pumpkin patch is "sincere." But what does that mean? What distinguishes a sincere patch from an insincere one? And what if someone else's patch is more sincere? If the Great Pumpkin never shows, that might not mean it doesn't exist. So, whether a belief is rational also depends partly on the likelihood that you will get the information you need and that it will accurately tell you what you need to know. In other words, you have to know the *risks* and be comfortable with them.

So, one promising alternative to the classical view of rationality is to say that a belief is rational just in case it is *responsible*. A belief is formed responsibly when we pay attention to the evidence but we also consider the value of the belief and the risks associated with believing it. It involves forming a belief carefully and with the right attitudes: we are interested in having a true belief, we form it under the right conditions (we are paying attention, the lighting is good, we aren't on strong medication, etc.), we are open to new evidence (like discovering that we were dreaming), we consider how valuable the belief is, and we consider the risks of being wrong.

Was Sally's belief that she should wait with Linus rational? Given how angry she is at the end of the night because she missed tricks-or-treats, it seems not. The value of learning whether the Great Pumpkin exists was low relative to other things she wanted, namely, to go trick-or-treating for the first time. Even though she wanted a true belief about the Great Pumpkin, it wasn't worth it to her to take the time to find out.

How can we tell whether we've balanced evidence, value, and risk well? This is not easy, but some philosophers suggest it requires what Aristotle called the *intellectual virtues*: intellectual *curiosity* to seek out evidence you don't have, intellectual *courage* to follow evidence where it leads, intellectual *humility* to admit you could be wrong, intellectual *charity* to listen to others when they disagree with you, intellectual, *self-knowledge* to know what you value and how strongly, and *conscientiousness* to assess risks accurately. According to this *virtue theory* of rational belief, if we practice these virtues regularly, the beliefs we adopt will be rational even if they turn out to be wrong.

Pumpkin-style Beliefs

Now we are in a better position to ask whether Linus's belief in the Great Pumpkin is rational and whether belief in God is anything like it. Let's call a "Pumpkin-style belief" any belief where the evidence is unfavorable. Evidence can be unfavorable for a number of reasons. One way is that the belief is *too vague* to be supported by evidence.

For example, some people believe their horoscopes, but horoscopes are typically so vague, that any number of events could be interpreted as confirming them (a problem known as "multiple endpoints"). Another way evidence can be unfavorable is that there is *not enough of it* to support a belief. For instance, if someone says that gremlins exist, you are rightly skeptical on the grounds that there is not enough evidence for them (even if they try to associate gremlins with some physical effect, such as telling you that gremlins explain how the internet works).

Yet another way is that there is significant *evidence against* the belief. For example, there are a handful of people who still believe the Earth is flat, despite substantial evidence to the contrary. And remember, just because a belief is pumpkin-style doesn't mean it is irrational. Other examples include very common beliefs like "celebrities die in threes," "everything happens for a reason," "we will never get a divorce," "I will beat this cancer," and "I will win this race." It's a further question whether any of these is irrational.

Belief in the Great Pumpkin is a pumpkin-style belief, and on the classic view of evidence, Linus's belief is clearly irrational. It's not obviously true, it's not based on his senses, and it doesn't follow from beliefs formed in either of these ways. But on the classic view, as we've seen, most of our beliefs are irrational. We could not ask Linus to give up his belief while we kept most of ours, as if he were irrational and we were not. On the other hand, according to the virtue theory of rationality, whether Linus's belief is rational depends on more than just his evidence (or lack thereof). It also depends on how he formed his belief. If he formed it in an intellectually virtuous way, then his belief is rational.

Unfortunately, Linus's belief fails on the virtue account, too. Not only does Linus have no evidence for the Great Pumpkin, he allows the belief to cause a rift between him and his friends, and it makes him miss out on other valuable things, like tricks-or-treats. He lacks intellectual humility because he tries to insulate himself from evidence against the Great Pumpkin (the caveat at the end of his letter). And he lacks the intellectual courage to update the strength of his belief after the Great Pumpkin doesn't show up: since the Great Pumpkin didn't show up, Linus should either give up his belief that his pumpkin patch is the most sincere or that the Great Pumpkin exists. But he isn't willing to do either. Rather than believing virtuously, Linus's belief is vicious (against virtue), and therefore, irrational.

Now consider the belief that an all-powerful, all-knowing, all-good being created the world and everything in it, and maintains the existence of all these things purely by the exercise of its will. This is the sort of being that many religious traditions have called *God*. Some argue that this is not a pumpkin-style belief, that, in fact, there is good evidence for the existence of God. This view has a long history called "natural theology," where philosophers attempt to offer evidence-based arguments for the existence of God. But this is controversial, and many philosophers contend that this evidence is, at best, incomplete. So, for the sake of argument, let's assume belief in God is a pumpkin-style belief. In this case, could belief in God be rational?

Saving (Some) Pumpkin-style Beliefs

Some philosophers say belief in God could be rational, as long as the belief is formed in a *properly* basic way. For instance, when Alvin Plantinga gives the example of beliefs about breakfast based on memory, he says that it is *properly basic*. By "properly basic," he means that it forms spontaneously under the right sorts of conditions. What are the right conditions? Mainly that you *actually* had pancakes and blueberries, you weren't dreaming at the time, your eyes and taste buds were working properly, and so on. Now, we can't always know whether all those sorts of conditions hold because we don't always know whether we are dreaming or whether our taste buds are working properly (we could be ill). But there is a way to know whether your belief about breakfast is responsible. That's where our virtue theory comes in.

Imagine you were raised in a rural community where everyone believes that the gas helium exists. You've never seen or touched anything you would call "helium," and it is not obvious to you that it exists. Nevertheless, everyone says that helium exists, and you see bottles labeled "helium" around town. Unfortunately, no one can tell you how they know helium exists. The best they can do is tell you that someone told them that it does and point to the bottles. Every now and then, someone will say they read in a book that helium exists. You cannot find one of these books or anyone who has seen helium directly, but the elders of the town bring you a balloon that floats in the air. They tell you the balloon floats because it is filled with helium and helium, they say, is lighter than regular air. They also inhale some of it to make funny sounds with their voices and explain that this is caused by helium.

Now, we can imagine that this is the sort of situation the *Peanuts* gang is in with respect to helium. Is it rational for them to believe that helium exists? The adults probably associate certain effects with helium, but they don't know why it works or even how they know the gas exists. And notice that it doesn't matter that the belief happens to be true. On the classical view, everyone in such a community is irrational. This is a pumpkin-style belief because there is not enough evidence for it. And, of course, this is very similar to how children come to believe in Santa Claus.

So, how does this all relate back to the question of God's existence? As we already saw, kids have a pretty good reason to believe in Santa Claus. People they respect and love tell them it's true, and their surrounding world seems to confirm it. The community that believes in helium also seems quite rational for the same reasons. Even if there is not enough evidence for it according to the classical view of rationality, it is possible that they formed the belief responsibly—listening only to those people they consider trustworthy and adequately knowledgeable, they belief is useful for engaging with others and their world, and they could be genuinely open to an alternative explanation for floating balloons and squeaky voices should new evidence arise.

Now imagine you were raised in a community where everyone believes in God and where everyone practices roughly the same religious tradition, whether it is Roman Catholicism, Mormonism, Orthodox Judaism, Sunni Islam, or some other theistic religion. In such communities, no one is likely able to give the philosophers' arguments for God's existence. Nevertheless, they were told about God by people they respect and trust, their world seems to corroborate their stories (they might say nature is orderly like an intelligent mind, and it is beautiful like an artist's work), and they are genuinely open to alternative explanations.

If someone were to believe in God in such a community for those reasons, the virtue theory suggests that belief is rational. This explains how someone's belief that God exists could be rational without evidence but not their belief in the Great Pumpkin. If anyone in that community were to believe in God the way Linus believes in the Great Pumpkin—irresponsibly—that belief would be irrational, too. But if they believe virtuously, then the belief is rational.

Does this mean that belief in the Great Pumpkin could be rational under some conditions? Interestingly, yes. If there were a community that believed in the Great Pumpkin like many cultures believe in helium and God, it could. But it also suggests that the more diverse a culture is, the less strongly rational such beliefs will be. If people with many different views about God talk with one another, it will be difficult to continue believing in God without evidence. Just as children have an increasing number of experiences that make it more difficult to believe in Santa Claus, most people have experiences that make it more difficult to believe in God (such as suffering, natural disasters, and the diversity of religious traditions). This doesn't mean that belief in God necessarily becomes irrational without evidence, but it should cause us to pay closer attention to the evidence and adjust our beliefs accordingly.

On reflection, *It's the Great Pumpkin, Charlie Brown!* turns out to be more than an entertaining children's story. It also raises important questions about what sorts of beliefs are rational. Linus, Sally, and the gang show us that signed contracts are not always good evidence, that romantic crushes can distract us from believing responsibly, and that we should never ignore evidence, even if there is more to rational belief than evidence alone.

5
Rhapsody on a Theme by Schroeder

RACHEL ROBISON-GREENE

The first time Schroeder appeared at his iconic piano in the *Peanuts* comic strip was on September 24th 1951.

This was not the first time that Schroeder, himself, appeared in the strip. In his first appearance, he is portrayed as a young baby, at least three or four years younger than the rest of the *Peanuts* gang. There are several strips in which Schroeder is used in sketches with punch lines about babies. It's not long, however, before Schroeder plops down in front of the instrument he will be associated with for the rest of the series.

Schulz has revealed that his daughter Meredith's toy piano served as the inspiration for Schroeder's turn to the life of music. He's a natural. In that iconic strip from 1951, Charlie Brown demonstrates how to play the piano for baby Schroeder.

> CHARLIE: [*playing the piano*] PLINK PLINK PLINK. See how easy it is, Schroeder? PLINK PLINK PLINK. The piano is a beautiful instrument if played properly. Now let's hear you play, huh, Schroeder?
>
> SCHROEDER: [*plays an extremely complicated composition*]
>
> CHARLIE: [*blushes*]

From that moment on, Schroeder develops an almost unnatural passion for playing the piano, even at the cost of many of the joys of childhood.

Oh, for a Muse of Fire!

Lucy Van Pelt's unrequited love for Schroeder is one of the most famous gags from the series. Panel after panel features Lucy, leaning against and sometimes even lying on Schroeder's piano, jabbering at him as he, oblivious, plays on. Though the most prominent, Lucy isn't the only girl in the *Peanuts* gang who's smitten by Schroeder. Frieda also makes some appearances leaning against the toy piano.

It's no secret that women tend to love musicians. Long before there was Beatlemania, there was Lisztomania. German composer Franz Liszt was the source of some hysteria with the ladies. They would collect his gloves, broken piano strings, and strands of hair. One woman even went so far as to make one of his used cigar stumps into a locket that she religiously wore around her neck thereafter.

Schroeder seems to attract the attention of the ladies in a similar way, particularly in the case of Lucy Van Pelt. Schroeder, at least at first, is oblivious. Lucy, meanwhile, hangs on his every word.

LUCY: What is that you're playing Schroeder?

SCHROEDER: This is "The Waltz of the Flowers," Lucy. It's from the "Nutcracker Suite."

LUCY: Sweet! He called me Sweet!! I've never been so happy in all of my life!

Lucy is jealous of Schroeder's singular focus on music. The piano itself becomes the object of her jealousy. At one point in 1969, she even throws the piano into the kite-eating tree in an effort to be rid of it for good. Unfortunately for Lucy, her actions do not have the intended effect. Schroeder is now singularly focused on the fact that his piano is gone. He pays no more attention to her now than he ever did.

At first, it seems that Schroeder has absolutely no interest in the kind of attention that Lucy pays to him. In fact, it irritates him. In a series of strips from May 1966, however, it becomes obvious that Schroeder appreciated Lucy even more than he, himself, ever realized. In that series, Lucy's father gets a new job, and the family moves away. Schroeder didn't realize that Lucy was serious about moving away, and he finds that he misses her. As he tries to play the pain away on his toy piano, Lucy's face appears in the sheet music in his head, and he exclaims, "Don't tell me I've grown accustomed to that face!"

At the end of that series of strips, Lucy and Linus move back to town. Schroeder is quite relieved when Lucy once more plops down on his piano, informing him, "YOUR SWEETIE'S BACK!"

In a strip from 1984, Schroeder even kisses her. Lucy baked a cupcake for Schroeder in celebration of Beethoven's birthday. Delighted that she remembered and, overcome with emotion, Schroeder plants one right on her cheek. Alas, this doesn't resolve the seemingly unrequited love. When Lucy turns, she sees Snoopy and mistakenly believes that he was the one who kissed her. She runs off in disgust.

LUCY: AAUGH! Dog lips!

SCHROEDER: No! Wait! Wait, Lucy, wait!

SNOOPY: [*thinking*] What's wrong with dog lips?

Apparently, Lucy was the muse that Linus never knew he had—a muse that can inspire him to create.

Why We Need Music

Without Music, Life Would be a Mistake

—FRIEDRICH NIETZSCHE

German philosopher Friedrich Nietzsche would approve of Schroeder's preference for music over more common pursuits. In Nietzsche's view, ordinary human beings are herd animals. They avoid self-mastery and self-creation, preferring instead to follow paths in life that have been carved out for them by others. For Nietzsche, the Judeo-Christian worldview is the most popular of these paths.

Human beings tend to have the values that they have because their religion tells them to. The values that Christianity endorses are, in Nietzsche's view, self-denying values that stifle real creativity. Consider, for example, a set of common "priestly" values—obedience, poverty, and chastity. Each of these values involves a rejection of aspects of human lives that, in many cases, lead to standard types of human pleasure and excellence.

Chastity requires depriving yourself of sex. Poverty requires you to deprive yourself of material comforts. Obedience requires you to deprive yourself of real control over your own life. In short, Christian values seem to require people to deprive themselves of the goods of this life in order to earn the rewards of some future life to come.

Nietzsche argues that humans need to make way for the next stage in human evolution. If they can get past their obedience to self-denying principles, they can move on to be the creative forces that they are capable of becoming. As we will see, this is a path that might just be possible for Schroeder.

To achieve the status of a true creator, individuals must live for this life, rather than for some life to come. Nietzsche proposes a test to determine whether we, as individuals, are truly living for this life. He asks us to imagine that a demon came to us in the middle of the night some night and informs us that

> This life, as thou livest it at present, and hast lived it, thou must live it once more, and also innumerable times; and there will be nothing new in it, but every pain and every joy and every thought and every sigh, and all the unspeakably small and great in thy life must come to thee again, and all in the same series and sequence—and similarly this spider and this moonlight among the trees, and similarly this moment, and I myself. The eternal sand-glass of existence will ever be turned once more, and thou with it, thou speck of dust!

In other words, you're being asked to imagine that a demon comes to you and tells you that you will live your life exactly as you have lived it—in every precise detail—over and over again, forever. You won't be aware that you're repeating it. If living your life in exactly the way you have lived it seems like a blessing—you would enjoy nothing more—then you truly are living for this life. You are living life to the fullest and you strive for excellence even when it seems difficult. You pass the test. If, upon reflection, you find that living your life the way you have lived it up to this point sounds terrible, you fail the test, and you need to change how you live your life accordingly.

The way to really live for this life is to become a creative force. When we reflect on our lives in light of the hypothetical Nietzsche has proposed, how many of us can say that we exercised our full potential for creation? How many of us have a novel or a piece of art inside us that we never bothered to bring into being?

To the extent that we create, we are gods ourselves. There is no one who is more powerful than a true creator. Schroeder acknowledges an idea much like this in a strip from April 12th 1954:

> CHARLIE: [*reading to Schroeder*] One day, the ruler of Prussia sent Beethoven a watch. "This is nothing but a cheap watch," said Beethoven angrily! "But remember," said a friend, "it is a gift from a king!" "I too am a king!" said Beethoven.
>
> SCHROEDER: That's telling 'em Beethoven!

In his work, *The Birth Of Tragedy*, Nietzsche claims that music is the most vibrant expression of creative force. Music alone can serve as a vehicle for wild, creative joy and exuberance and expression of the human experience. The philosopher Arthur Schopenhauer heavily influenced Nietzsche's work. He contends that music can, better than anything else, expose us to the true nature of the world. In this sense, music can do what even language cannot.

Nietzsche says that

> all phenomena, compared with it, are but symbols: hence language, as the organ and symbol of phenomena, cannot at all disclose the innermost essence of music; language can only be in superficial contact with music when it attempts to imitate music; while the profoundest significance of the latter cannot be brought one step nearer to us by all the eloquence of lyric poetry. (*Birth of Tragedy*, p. 38)

One of the most memorable scenes from *A Charlie Brown Christmas* is the Christmas dance. Schroeder, accompanied by Pigpen on the bass and Snoopy on the guitar, plays the now iconic song, while the *Peanuts* gang (sans Charlie Brown) dances merrily on the stage. Nietzsche has much to say in *The Birth of Tragedy* about communities like this coming together to express themselves and to unify in music and dance. "In song and in dance man exhibits himself as a member of a higher community: he has forgotten how to walk and speak, and is on the point of taking a dancing flight into the air" (p. 27). This seems like an apt description of the *Peanuts* crew—they dance so merrily that their very faces disappear into the air!

These philosophical reflections infuse some of the *Peanuts* strips with additional humor. In a strip from July 18th 1954, Schroeder attempts to use Charlie Brown as a muse. He wants to capture Charlie Brown's personality in song:

SCHROEDER: I appreciate your coming over to help me Charlie Brown . . . The first thing we do is get you on a stool to sit on . .

CHARLIE: ?

SCHROEDER: This is something I learned from Virgil Thompson . . . You sit right there, see, and then I'll paint your musical portrait.

CHARLIE: Oh, I get it! You'll try to capture my personality in music . . . right?

SCHROEDER: Right . . . are you ready?

CHARLIE: I'm ready . . . This is very flattering! Mine is a personality that will probably inspire a heroic symphony . . . [*pause*] . . . I don't hear a thing . . . ? . . . [*blushes*]

SCHROEDER: [*running away*] !

CHARLIE: [*blushes harder*] Sigh.

This strip suggests that even music, the great expresser of the inexpressable, the creative force that can show us the true nature of the world, even combined with the musical genius of toddler prodigy Schroeder, can make nothing of ol' wishy-washy, blockheaded Charlie Brown. Of course, we diehard fans of the series know what his song would truly sound like. We know from watching Charlie Brown cartoon specials every holiday season. That song transcends words. "Baa ba ba baa ba ba, baa, baa . . .? See?

Roll Over Beethoven

If a member of the *Peanuts* gang wanted to start a conversation with Schroeder, they would be wise to discuss his favorite topic—Beethoven. He finds little else to be interesting or worthwhile. In a strip from December 26th 1954, Charlie Brown visits Schroeder's house to see what his friend got for Christmas. It seems that Schroeder was on the "nice" list that year, because he received many gifts. He shows Charlie Brown a new piano, a new bust of Beethoven to set on his piano as inspiration, a Beethoven sweatshirt, a twelve-volume biography of Beethoven in comic book form, a Beethoven ballpoint pen, and a year's supply of Beethoven bubblegum. He also directs Charlie Brown to a brand new train set that he received for Christmas. "Now what in the world am I going to do with an electric train!" he bemoans.

In a strip from December, 1953, we find out that Schroeder holds Beethoven in such high esteem, that his idol's birthday is, for him, a yearly holiday.

CHARLIE: Come on Schroeder, we'll be late for school.

SCHROEDER: I'm not going today.

CHARLIE: You're not going?! Why not?

SCHROEDER: This is Beethoven's birthday!

Every human being has role models—people they look up to and whom they seek to emulate. For Schroeder, this person is obviously Beethoven. Nietzsche, too, had great respect for Beethoven. He uses Beethoven's music to illustrate his idea that even the best of lyrical language cannot express what music is capable of expressing:

> We again and again have occasion to observe how a symphony of Beethoven compels the individual hearers to use figurative speech, though the appearance presented by a collocation of the different pictorial world generated by a piece of music may be never so fantastically diversified and even contradictory. (*Birth of Tragedy*, pp. 37–38)

But Nietzsche's philosophy has one more important lesson for Schroeder. He must be careful that he doesn't let his respect for the composer get in the way of his own personal development as a creator of music. The true creator, the true Nietzschean superman, must not merely imitate the creations of others. He must bring his own art into being.

Lucy can inspire Schroeder. Beethoven can serve as his role model, in much the same way that Wagner was a role model to Nietzsche himself in the writer's youth. There is nothing wrong with recognizing the good in others and integrating that goodness into your own character. But Schroeder must do more than play the symphonies of Beethoven; he must use his genius to create his own compositions.

He is shown doing this, from time to time, though he's shown far more often playing Beethoven. When he comes into his own as an artist, future musicians will idolize him the way he does Beethoven.

As Charlie Brown says, "You've heard of Bach, Beethoven, and Brahms? Well from now on it's going to be Schubert, Schumann, and Schroeder!"

6
Anti-Psychiatric Help 5¢—
The Doctor Is IN

HEIDI SAMUELSON

Lucy Van Pelt is not a licensed psychiatrist. She does not have the medical or scientific background required to practice psychiatry, though she does offer "psychiatric help" for a nickel.

Her advice is never helpful, often insensitive, and she seems opportunistic when she refuses to give advice without payment in advance. More damning of Lucy's practice, Charlie Brown—her most regular patient—doesn't seem to feel any better after receiving her "advice." You have to wonder if maybe Lucy is purposefully undermining psychiatry with her booth. Maybe Lucy Van Pelt is actually an anti-psychiatrist.

The term "anti-psychiatry," coined in 1967 by David Cooper, covers a wide range of views. An "anti-psychiatry" position does not necessarily mean that mental illness is bogus or that there isn't a benefit to various therapies. Rather, anti-psychiatry views are critical of the sometimes dangerous or ineffective ways that psychiatry is practiced.

Three of anti-psychiatry's major criticisms of psychiatry are:

1. that there's a potentially-harmful power relation between the doctor and patient, which Lucy demonstrates by being something of a bully;

2. that treatment is often ineffective, even harmful, and doesn't ultimately cure or help the patient—case in point, Lucy's advice looks like a bargain, but sometimes it makes Charlie feel worse;

3. that although it purports to be grounded in objective, measurable conditions, psychiatry cannot be objective, which Lucy shows by betraying the profession and giving advice based on her opinions.

What has emerged out of the anti-psychiatry of the 1960s and 1970s is a "critical psychiatry," which no longer calls itself "anti-psychiatry" but questions the practice of psychiatry from a more social perspective.

Some critics coming from within the field of psychiatry suggest a more holistic way to approach mental suffering—taking into account non-biological conditions that affect patients, trying to understand patients' experiences, creating a more open dialogue between patients and doctors, and, particularly in the case of depression, using less general diagnostic criteria.

Ultimately what we Charlie Browns of the world can learn from Lucy through Charles Schulz's famous converted lemonade stand is to stay critical and recognize what *not* to look for in psychiatric treatment.

That'll Be Five Cents, Please

Pretend you have decided to seek out psychiatric help because you're feeling depressed—not just sad about losing a baseball game or because the Little Red-Haired Girl doesn't know you exist, but because you feel a general despair about life. Over the course of *Peanuts'* almost fifty-year run, this happens to Charlie Brown numerous times.

One criticism of psychiatry is that it depends on power dynamics, which have been used as a means of manipulation. Indeed, psychiatric research has a troubling history. Psychiatric techniques were used as an oppressive political tool in Nazi Germany with the practice of eugenics to "weed out mental defects" from the population. In the US, Project

MKUltra was a CIA-sponsored research program that did experiments in engineering human behavior by manipulating test subjects' mental states in an attempt to improve interrogation techniques. A neighborhood psychiatry stand is clearly not at this sinister level, but the history of manipulation casts a dark shadow, even over Lucy's booth.

In a therapeutic setting, there is a power dynamic between the psychiatrist and patient. A patient must typically demonstrate a certain amount of dependence and vulnerability in order to talk about their personal, mental, and behavioral problems, and this puts the psychiatrist in a position of power over them. Some argue that this is inherent to the therapeutic setting, because the patient has sought out the authority of the psychiatrist. But, for effective therapy, the patient must trust that the psychiatrist will listen to them and take seriously what they are saying without ridicule, coercion, or harm. Charlie certainly opens himself up to Lucy and voluntarily seeks out her psychiatry booth. Lucy, however, proves the critics right by being coercive and sometimes downright threatening.

> CHARLIE BROWN: Well, I appreciate the help you've given me. I was wondering, though, if I should get a second opinion.
>
> LUCY: Only if you don't mind my beating you over the head with that stool you're sitting on!
>
> CHARLIE BROWN: I guess first opinions are pretty good.

Threat of bodily harm is an extreme reaction of a psychiatrist, and it does not mean that therapy is necessarily abusive, but it does demonstrate that it *can* be. In a genuine therapeutic setting, we would hope the psychiatrist wouldn't call the patient a "blockhead" or "wishy-washy," but these are insults regularly given by Lucy to Charlie both in and out of the psychiatry booth.

In one panel, Lucy says, "You're really not much use to anyone, Charlie Brown! You're weak, and dumb, and boring, and hopeless!!" When Charlie goes to Lucy for help, he accepts her authority, and in doing so, he also accepts her insults.

In one strip, Charlie opens up to Lucy about his fears, specifically his fear of being boring, and she responds by confirming his fear exactly.

> CHARLIE BROWN: I have a great fear of being boring. I also have a great fear of being bored. What's the most bored you've ever been?
>
> LUCY: Besides right now?

Lucy's insults would be harsh coming from anyone. But by accepting Lucy as an authority figure, it seems very likely Charlie would believe and internalize her words.

Another example of Lucy demonstrating her power over Charlie to his detriment happens in the infamous football gag, where Lucy holds the football for Charlie to kick, only to pull it away at the last second, causing Charlie to fall. Lucy might justify her continual pulling the football away from Charlie as teaching him a valuable lesson about trust. But it seems that this isn't the case. In the very first strip in which Lucy pulls the ball away, she claims it was because she didn't want the ball to get dirty, and the gag continues to be an example of Charlie putting his trust in Lucy only to have her take it away.

Lucy is self-absorbed, and beyond the "doctor-patient" relationship, she often lords herself over Charlie (and the rest of the *Peanuts* gang). In one series of comic strips, Lucy insists that the year is "hers," and she puts down anyone who criticizes it. She says to her brother Linus, "I can feel it! I've been waiting for this year all of my life, and I know this is it!" Then she shouts, "I hereby declare that this is my year!!" Linus turns to Snoopy in the final panel and says, "Maybe if we're lucky, she'll let us have a few Tuesdays . . ." In another day's strip, Charlie Brown ask her, "Where does that leave the rest of us?" Lucy replies, "Nowhere! Stay out of my year!!!"

Lucy's need to assert herself as the focus of an entire year might just be masking her own issues and insecurities. She does tell Snoopy that the previous year wasn't a very good one for her, but she shares this with the dog and not one of her human peers, showing that she's unwilling to express the kind of vulnerability she expects from her patients when she sits behind the psychiatry booth. Lucy's constant exercise of power legitimizes the first criticism of psychiatry, and, because she seems to enjoy her power, certainly makes her a bad psychiatrist.

Good Grief!

In the very first appearance of Lucy's psychiatry booth in the comic strips, Charlie opens by saying, "I have deep feelings of depression . . . What can I do about this?" Lucy's response is, "Snap out of it! Five cents, please."

The first problem with Lucy's response is that it doesn't even remotely recognize or validate Charlie's feelings; in fact, she throws Charlie's depression right back in his face. The second problem is that she demands payment for advice that is ineffective.

At worst, Lucy's "advice" could make Charlie feel hopeless—exacerbating his symptoms of depression. But the practice of psychiatry has an unfortunate history of "treatments" that were harmful to patients—electroshock therapy, isolation, straightjackets, ice water baths, fever induction, bleeding, insulin comas, lobotomies (cutting out sections of the brain), and trephination (drilling holes in the skull). There's even a "psychiatric survivors" movement, started by former patients who experienced abuse at the hands of psychiatric practice. Their aim is to give power back to patients and advocate for patients' rights.

Contemporary critics of psychiatry see the current influence of the pharmaceutical industry, which makes big bucks on drugs that purport to correct chemical imbalances in the brain, as following in the footsteps of these harmful treatments that were once also considered scientifically valid.

There are numerous accusations against the pharmaceutical industry for distorting mental health, including perpetuating the idea that brain chemicals are easily measurable and that there is a particular "balance" that defines mental stability.

The American Psychological Association reports that in 2010 Americans spent more than $16 billion on antipsychotics, $11 billion on antidepressants, and $7 billion for drugs to treat attention-deficit hyperactivity disorder. Drugs are often over-prescribed, and a study by the Centers for Disease Control and Prevention suggests that many are prescribed without the patients being evaluated by a mental-health professional—not even one with a makeshift booth!

The psychiatric drug segment of the pharmaceutical industry has expanded beyond the therapeutic setting, beyond psychiatry booths, into a giant industry that involves marketing, lobbying, and legislation, realms far outside issues of the mental well-being of individuals. The rising cost (and questionable effectiveness) of pharmaceuticals makes five cents of bogus advice seem fairly innocuous—and possibly just as useful as the placebo effect, which some critics of drug treatments say is just as effective as common antidepressants.

Critics of psychiatry suggest that the increase in the use of antidepressants, particularly in the US, indicates that this type of treatment doesn't seem to be "curing" anyone. The expansion of the pharmaceutical industry has gone to direct-to-consumer advertising and even to financial backing of advocacy groups that promote pharmaceuticals as the only treatment for conditions like depression. While antidepressants seem to work for some patients, the pharmaceutical industry clearly has a stake in more people being diagnosed and subsequently treated with their drugs. It's not hard to imagine Pfizer sponsoring Lucy's booth.

Recommended treatments for depression and other mental illnesses still include a combination of medication and psychotherapy, like cognitive behavioral therapy, even in cases of mental illness that are initially responsive to drugs.

But the effectiveness of psychotherapy is also suspect. The benefit of therapy depends on the relationship between the therapist and the patient. Years of comic strips show that Lucy is probably not the best option for Charlie, but often patients are stuck with what they can afford, because therapy is not always covered by health insurance—and Lucy is certainly affordable.

In spite of her flaws, sometimes it does seem that Lucy puts some thought into Charlie's problems. In one strip, Lucy sits behind her booth talking to Charlie and says, "I've been thinking about your case, Charlie Brown . . . Your fear of being alone is not unusual . . . What you need is a dog!" In the final panel, Snoopy appears beside Lucy thinking, "Who do you think *I* am, Kermit the Frog?!"

Although she's validating Charlie's feelings of fear, unfortunately for her credibility as a psychiatrist, her advice is a non-starter. Yes, there has been research that shows that caring for a pet has therapeutic value, but Charlie already has a dog. Lucy does not pay attention to her patient, making her therapeutic setting not open or communicative, reiterating the anti-psychiatric point that treatment is often ineffective.

In addition to being ineffective, Lucy's treatment of Charlie might actually make him feel worse. Nevertheless, and why I suggest she might be a closet anti-psychiatrist, sometimes Lucy seems aware of this.

> **CHARLIE BROWN:** Do you think I can ever become a mature and well-adjusted person?
>
> **LUCY:** For a question like that, I have to be paid in advance.
>
> **CHARLIE BROWN:** In advance?! Why?
>
> **LUCY:** Because I don't think you're going to like the answer.

Lucy's realistic approach to Charlie's question supports the idea that she is problematizing the psychiatric practice. She doesn't think what she can offer Charlie in response to his question will have the positive effect on him that he is seeking in asking for psychiatric help.

Everybody Is Entitled to My Opinion

One of the most famous criticisms of psychiatry that came out of the anti-psychiatry movement is that it is overly medicalized. Because mental illness involves thoughts, feelings, behaviors, and relationships, it cannot be an objective, scientific matter like "having a bodily disease or not."

The well-known critic of psychiatry Thomas Szasz famously suggested that you need a whole different set of terms to describe a bodily illness from a mental problem, so "illness" isn't even the right term for a mental disorder that cannot be reduced to a problem in the body. Though some mental illnesses do correlate to known physiological conditions, generally, you can't look *only* for something like an observable virus, a physical wound, or malignant cells—the way medical professionals do with physical ailments—in order to diagnose a mental disorder. Diagnostic criteria go beyond physical symptoms, and patients seek help from therapists, psychologists—or psychiatry booths—that is, from non-medical professionals.

Diagnosis of mental illness also depends on a subjective assessment of behavioral symptoms, including patient self-reporting, as Charlie Brown demonstrates, which is inherently non-objective. Perhaps psychiatry doesn't need to be objective, but there seems to be a desire among both psychiatrists and patients for objective, measurable diagnostic tests and pharmaceuticals that will treat and cure mental illnesses and solidify trust in the psychiatric profession. Patients want their mental disorders to be viewed the same way as physical illnesses, but that doesn't seem to be the type of thing that psychiatry can really do because of the very nature of mental illness.

Attempts to standardize and categorize mental illness have been made, particularly with the Diagnostic and Statistical Manual of Mental Disorders (DSM), first published in 1952 and currently in its fifth version. The publication has been criticized for its lack of objectivity, as well as its inclusion of conditions not commonly considered pathological, including homosexuality, which was categorized as a mental disorder until 1973. It is possible that Lucy is unwittingly protesting traditional psychiatric diagnoses, because she never identifies anything physically or measurably wrong with Charlie, and she never mentions the DSM, other than indirectly via her knowledge of particular phobias.

Though Lucy doesn't come right out and say she rejects objectivity, her "treatments" are never medical in nature. She doesn't even give much thought to her patient's physical symptoms at all, although you might expect that from a more subjective method of treatment like talk therapy. But, Lucy's "treatments" are only given in terms of advice—advice that is not tailored to the particulars of her patient's situation. Sometimes her advice is ineffective, and even circular, and it always seems to come from her own personal perspective, not her patient's.

> CHARLIE BROWN: What can you do when you don't fit in? What can you do when life seems to be passing you by?

> LUCY: Follow me. I want to show you something. See the horizon over there? See how big this world is? See how much room there is for everybody? Have you ever seen any other worlds?

> CHARLIE BROWN: No.

> LUCY: As far as you know this is the only world there is . . . right?

> CHARLIE BROWN: Right.

> LUCY: There are no other worlds for you to live in . . . right?

> CHARLIE BROWN: Right.

> LUCY: WELL, LIVE IN IT, THEN!

Charlie is tossed upside down by the force of Lucy's voice. To add insult to injury, she adds in the final panel, "Five cents, please."

The trouble with psychiatric practice is that if there is not a laboratory test that can be performed to confirm the presence of a mental illness, or if there are no objective standards to determine the severity of a mental illness, then diagnosis requires interpretation of feelings and behavior. By acting as if her opinion is an effective treatment, Lucy is effectively rejecting traditional "objective" therapies and perhaps recognizing that objectivity is impossible. Unfortunately for Charlie, he doesn't get the help he's seeking.

We shouldn't blame Lucy for her inability to treat Charlie. She is a child and clearly has not had any formal training. Not to mention, Charlie deals with existential crises that are well beyond his years. Lucy ultimately never gives Charlie Brown a psychiatric diagnosis. She might just be a lousy "psychiatrist," but if we give her the benefit of the doubt, she looks more like a critic of psychiatry but one who still seems to want to help. Lucy might have developed better therapeutic techniques by thinking about mental illness differently and looking at a fuller, more complex, situated human experience.

Dreading One Day at a Time

While Dr. Thomas Szasz takes the most extreme view in denouncing psychiatry as a dangerous and immoral pseudoscience, there are other critics of psychiatry who suggest psychiatry should focus more on the notion that the mind and body are connected and can influence one another. Other critics suggest mental health should not ignore that human beings are situated in a culture that influences their thoughts and behaviors.

Some critics of psychiatry think the problem with psychiatry is that it attempts to make diagnoses based on too vague a set of factors, like those listed in the DSM. A driving idea behind all of these critics is that a person does not exist in isolation, so social conditions influence one's mental state.

It isn't just Lucy who bullies Charlie. Patty and Violet routinely put him down and make fun of the size of his head. Charlie is convinced that no one likes him and admits to having a hard time "being Charlie Brown." He is affected by the world around him, and his friends and classmates notice and seem to pick on him because of it.

In his *History of Madness*, Michel Foucault traces back ideas of "madness" through periods of history where people labeled "mad" were romanticized in one era, then treated like criminals in another. He points out that in modern psychiatry, people who were once excluded from society are now treated as a technical problem that can be fixed with analysis and examination by "experts." His point is to show that "madness" is affected by historical, cultural context, and it is important to remain critical of practices that have changed over time, because they will continue to change.

Foucault sees psychiatric problems as difficult and contradictory social problems that are open to analysis. Current psychiatric practices have emerged out of a particular historical situation that could have been otherwise, and this has led critics to challenge the authority of so-called "experts." It's almost as if anyone can set up a booth and call themselves a psychiatrist.

The upshot is that treatment doesn't need to be based on some kind of "objective" standard to be effective. If a pill helps a patient and it is properly prescribed, then the patient should take the medication. But it is short-sided to think that this is the *only* valid method of psychiatric treatment or that it should not occur without also looking at social conditions or having an open dialogue between a therapist and a patient. Lucy is definitely not an expert in any school of psychiatric thought—she seemingly never psychoanalyzes Charlie, never provides cognitive behavioral therapy, and doesn't try to prescribe him drugs. She is actually an anti-psychiatrist of a sort, rejecting common psychiatric techniques by demonstrating how ineffective they are.

Even though Lucy's advice is unhelpful, the advice she *attempts* to give points to something more like "mindfulness therapy." That is, underneath her aggressive tactics, she suggests that Charlie can find help through building connections to the world or becoming aware of his thoughts and accepting them without attaching to them—a type of treatment sometimes used to prevent a relapse of depression. Her alternative form of therapy might be another piece of evidence that makes Lucy a secret anti-psychiatrist, but due to her exercise of power and her inability to listen to Charlie, she doesn't seem like the best candidate to provide this kind of therapy.

It ends up being Linus who, as Charlie's friend and confidant, offers Charlie a new perspective without threatening or bullying him. Linus says, "You need a new outlook, Charlie Brown. Try to look at your life as if it were a book, and each day as if it were a page in that book . . ." And, "I guess it's wrong always to be worrying about tomorrow. Maybe we should think only about today . . ."

At one point, Charlie almost adopts this line of thinking—in his own way: "I've developed a new philosophy. I only dread one day at a time." Perhaps Charlie Brown will never be the epitome of positivity; he wrestles with a dark view of the world and is pessimistic about his place in it. "Sometimes I lie awake at night, and I ask, 'Where have I gone wrong'. Then a voice says to me, 'This is going to take more than one night'." It might be that traditional psychiatry just doesn't work on Charlie because he has what Irvin D. Yalom refers to as "existential depression," which is a depression that arises when someone confronts the four "givens of existence": death, freedom, isolation, and meaninglessness. This is different from looking at depression as a mere chemical imbalance in the brain and does not exactly match the DSM criteria.

Another possibility is that Charlie might simply be reacting to sadness stressors—like the mocking and ridicule he endures from his peers. Allan V. Horowitz and Jerome C. Wakefield have suggested in *The Loss of Sadness* that depression, while a legitimate psychiatric condition, has been over-diagnosed, because the psychiatric profession has taken non-pathological experiences of human sadness and classified them as abnormal, largely in an effort by the DSM to define disorders with a minimal amount of criteria that don't distinguish between reasonable reactions to stressors and enduring pathological conditions.

These alternative therapies and diagnoses follow in the footsteps of the "anti-psychiatry" movement. Though there are some extreme positions that want to eradicate psychiatry, what we see from examining Lucy's psychiatry booth is a healthy skepticism and a critique from within psychiatry itself. Over-exercising authority, ineffective treatment, inappropriate reliance on pharmaceuticals, and narrow diagnostic tools are all criticisms of psychiatry that can be found if you take seriously Lucy's rather unprofessional attempt at psychiatry.

Though she is not well-suited to give it, Lucy's "therapy" points to alternative methods of understanding and treating depression of the sort that Charlie seems to have—of course, we'd need to know more about Charlie's state of mind, feelings, and behavior to diagnose him.

Ultimately, the point of Charles Schulz's comic strip might be that there is no solution to the dissatisfaction and dread that comes with examining human existence the way Charlie does. Lucy's ineffectiveness at psychiatry might simply be a parody, acting as a foil to a more important point: Charlie Brown was willing to be vulnerable and give a voice to his sadness, destigmatizing the need for psychiatric or therapeutic help, whether it comes from traditional methods or a nickel of anti-psychiatric advice.

III

How Good Is Grief?

7
Life, Liberty, and the Pursuit of a Warm Blanket

SEBASTIAN SCHUHBECK

I have two wonderful grown up daughters, who, when they were still little, had their favorite toy animals. For our daily bedtime routines those animals became as indispensable as they were for playing in the sandbox in our garden or for going on vacation trips.

Although I knew from classes in developmental psychology I had taken at university that English pediatrician and psychoanalyst Donald Winnicott calls such toys "transitional objects," I allowed my daughters to call them by their utterly unscientific names "Bunny" and "Bearie." Surprisingly, the names I had picked, "Transitional object number one" and "Transitional object number two," somehow didn't catch on with them.

By now it's sufficiently clear that this anecdote is just a moderately clever attempt to avoid opening this chapter with a clumsy line like "Well, what's the deal with Linus and his security blanket?"

When Does My Brain Know It Has a Mind (or Vice Versa)?

Donald Winnicott's theory about transitional objects like "Bunny," "Bearie," and Linus's security blanket refers to particular early sequences in a child's development. In the first months infants see themselves and their mother as a whole, as a unit; there is no difference between "me" and "not-me," between the internal world of needs, feelings and thoughts and the external world. When the baby is hungry, somehow, almost automatically, there comes food and this need is met.

And remember: For the baby this all seems to be going on within one closed, unified reality. "I experience this somewhat unpleasant feeling of hunger, and I can also make it go away—cool!" This automatism creates the illusion of "subjective omnipotence" for the baby: "The world is obviously good insofar as I can 'control' it, I can trust it. It is not a dreadful place in which my survival is highly questionable."

After a couple of months, however, the baby becomes aware of the separation between "me" and "not-me." At the same time the infant realizes that most of those many "not-me" objects are beyond its reach and range of influence. In the baby's mind the reassuring feeling of being omnipotent has to make way for the bitter insight that it is dependent on others: Sometimes mommy is here at an instant, sometimes she isn't. Naturally, this raises the quite fundamental question for the child if that one "significant other" can be relied on.

This is why the baby's mother brings a third item into the me-plus-mommy-equation: the transition object. The baby's reasoning will go somewhere along the line: "Aha, every time one of my primary needs is met, this object is near. There must be some connection!" And from such repeated observations the child subconsciously draws the conclusion that there must be a cause-effect-relationship between all the good and motherly things in its life and that object.

Okay, we could also say that the baby is conditioned through a repeated stimulus-response-pattern, but then the image of Pavlov's dog would come up, and we don't like the idea that our kids can be manipulated like dogs—aaugh!!! (Even though it's true sometimes.)

So, during this transition between the child's perception of the first months ("I AM the world") and the realization "There is a person who BRINGS and means the world to me," a transitional object gets emotionally charged like a sort of warranty card that mom is gonna be back and everything is going to be just fine—voilà, the security blanket.

You and That Stupid Blanket

With Donald Winnicott's theory we can now explain *how* Linus developed his attachment to his blanket in the first twelve months of his life. Looking at the history of the *Peanuts* cartoons, we're left totally clueless, however, as to why he's still so extraordinarily dependent on this comfort object, even though he's already going to school and all the other kids of the *Peanuts* gang have apparently emancipated themselves from such obvious ties to their infant years.

An overly simplistic answer might sound like "Well, he's just a weird kid!" or, if we put it a little less elegantly, "Linus seems to have a lot of unresolved issues!" But before we drop the "weirdo"-hammer on Linus, let's pursue this question more benevolently. Like Charlie Brown for example, when he comes to his friend's defense in *Happiness Is a Warm Blanket, Charlie Brown* (2011) and in *The Peanuts Movie* (2015), after Lucy—like so many times before—has tried to rid her brother of his habit:

> You know, Lucy, I have to admit, I see some value in this blanket business. It seems to put him in a mood for contemplation. I imagine it quiets his mind so he can really think about things. In fact, I think a lot of your problems would be solved, Lucy, if you had a blanket. Maybe if you had a blanket, you wouldn't be so crabby. And so mean-spirited. And so . . . [*Lucy slaps him*] . . . quick-tempered.

First of all: Ouch, that hurt! And I'm not talking about Charlie, but about Lucy. He has obviously touched a rather sore spot there. In a rather subtle way, Charlie makes Lucy realize that she has issues, too, and that her intolerance of Linus's little "weakness" is a case of "Judge not, lest ye be judged," or if you prefer a religiously neutral saying, a case of "The pot calling the kettle black." From a humor-theoretical point of view "Sparky" Schulz has done a great job here: "Defending" herself against being called mean-spirited and quick-tempered by slapping Charlie is of course utterly paradoxical; the viewer realizes this incongruity and feels amused.

But let's focus on a second aspect here: The question how Linus's blanket "works"—assuming, of course, that the immediate function of a transition object is no longer given, since he is already too old for that. How does it quiet his mind? On a more general level we can also ask how all sorts of lucky charms, talismans, esoteric objects and superstitious rituals survive in an age of reason and science. The answer is "magical thinking."

It's Magic

"Magical thinking" means seeing cause-effect relationships between actions and events which cannot be justified by reason and observation, with the underlying assumption that some mysterious "powers" are responsible for such effects. And at the same time people who cling to such magical thinking subscribe to the idea of somehow being able to "tap into" those secret powers and harnessing them in a particular way or to protect themselves against them.

At first glance Linus's security blanket seems to fall under the rubric of a stupid superstition. Not so fast, though! Psychologists and anthropologists have studied superstitious behavior in sports and, guess what?, apart from the fact that it is rather common, it seems to "work," too. At least to a certain degree and of course not due to some supernatural intervention.

So, how does Linus "profit" from carrying his blanket with him? George Gmelch from the University of San Francisco has studied superstitious behavior in baseball for decades and in his article *Baseball Magic* he explains how some of our best athletes have various superstitions and he categorizes them into three groups: fetishes, rituals, and taboos. But please, I can't state this clearly enough, a fetish, as meant here in the context of (pseudo-) religious beliefs and superstitions, has absolutely no sexual connotation. So, gentlemen, drop those mental images of fishnet-stockings, latex, high-heels or whatever else may cross your mind at this moment—geez!

A fetish in this context is simply a charm, an object that embodies "supernatural" power and can transfer it to its owner simply by being close. The underlying belief is that this supernatural power will somehow "rub off" through contact; it's "contagious" so to speak. This is why this sort of magical thinking belongs into the first of the two major categories of magic: "contagious magic." Superstitious athletes will insist on wearing specific lucky socks or jerseys for example, and sometimes even refuse to let them be cleaned for fear that their good fortune might be washed away. Linus's security blanket clearly falls into the fetish category.

There is a second category of magic: "sympathetic magic" or "imitative magic." In this case the supernatural power is harnessed—as the name already implies—by imitation or by some sort of resemblance between, let's say, an object and a person. Piercing a voodoo doll to hurt the person it resembles is an example for this kind of magic. So, next time someone tells you that walnuts are good for your brain, remember that this is magical thinking on the basis that the nut's shell very roughly resembles the shape of a brain. Not its size, hopefully!

And when in some cultures men with erectile dysfunction consider powder made from an elephants tusk or other phallic symbols to be helpful, well, then again we see that same magical thinking at work and poachers in Africa making money from this superstition.

When some players have curious routines or rituals—sometimes quite elaborate ones—then it's a case of imitative magic. They did something meaningful the last time they won. "Well, then let's do the same thing again and victory will be ours." And regardless if you're an athlete or Joe Six-Pack . . . routines have the additional effect that they are, if nothing else, comforting since they bring at least some order into a world in which people otherwise have little control.

Sweetest Taboo

For superstitious people rituals and fetishes are just one way of coping with the overburdening uncertainty of the world (or just a baseball game). They give clear instructions on what people are supposed to do (or to possess) to guarantee a desirable outcome. But magical thinking can also tell you what *not* to do in specific situations, and in this case we speak of a "taboo."

The word taboo comes from the Polynesian language and means "prohibited" or "forbidden." It was introduced into the English language by Captain James Cook, after he had visited Tonga in 1771, where he observed that the natives painstakingly avoided touching certain objects because—as they later explained—they were "taboo." The "power" of a taboo is based on the belief that it is either too sacred, and so touching it would compromise its sacredness, or it's simply too dangerous or evil. Breaking a rule that something is taboo, regardless of whether it is too sacred or too evil, means bad luck. For professional baseball players such a taboo may mean not to step on certain parts of the field or not to touch certain objects or even to say certain words. Just talking about a "no-hitter," for example, while one is in progress may already be too much for the magic spell and destroy all hopes of achieving this goal—"Don't jinx it, man!"

Linus has a moment of breaking one of his taboos in *It's the Great Pumpkin, Charlie Brown* (1966). Remember when he and Sally are sitting in the pumpkin patch waiting for the Great Pumpkin? Near the end of that episode all the other kids drop by to see how that Great Pumpkin evening was going for the two of them . . . just when Sally bursts into a frustrated fury after realizing that this whole evening was simply an enormous waste of time and she was robbed of her chance to go trick-or-treating. While they are all leaving Linus shouts after them:

Hey, aren't you gonna wait and greet the Great Pumpkin?— Huh?—It won't be long now! If the Great Pumpkin comes I'll still put in a good word for you! [*And now he realizes that he has just used a taboo word.*] Good grief! I said "if"! I meant "when" he comes!—I'm doomed. One little slip like that can cause the Great Pumpkin to pass you by. Oh, Great Pumpkin, where are you?

Yes, the Great Pumpkin seems to be a strict but fair pumpkin. Faithful believers will be rewarded, but skeptics will be punished by not appearing in front of them. Notice the implicit logic here? Linus has created a nice and impenetrable line of defense for himself: My belief that the Great Pumpkin will rise from a pumpkin patch on Halloween is absolutely true. Should he, however, not appear as expected, this would not at all prove that he doesn't exist, but only that I didn't believe in him strongly enough.

Seriously, Is Your Brain Out of Your Mind?

Alright! So all those rituals, taboos and fetishes come from magical thinking. People like Linus, who perceive the world as uncertain, unpredictable and beyond their control, get the illusion of control from magic objects and rituals. But before we return to Linus's security blanket in a bit, I would like to ask you a seemingly simple and yet deeply philosophical question: Now that you're reading this text . . . who's actually doing the reading?

And, by the way, the answer "Well, *me* of course!" doesn't count. Your next answer is probably going to be "My brain!" Yeah, . . . but are you sure that your thoughts and your brain are really identical? Your next guess is probably going to be "My mind?" Bingo! But then we still have to solve the riddle of what "the mind" is. Or where, for that matter.

The so-called "mind-body problem" has troubled philosophers for hundreds of years and, regrettably, the jury's still out on this question. The ancient Egyptians believed that the heart was the place where the mind was, even though they knew that the brain existed. (Mummifying dead Pharaohs had promoted their knowledge of the human anatomy quite a bit). In a short treatise *On the Sacred Disease* about the treatment of epilepsy the Greek physician and philosopher Hippocrates (around 400 B.C.) wrote that

> Men ought to know that from nothing else but the brain come joys, delights, laughter and sports, and sorrows, griefs . . .

Okay, we knew all along that Linus's brain must somehow be involved when his body craves for his security blanket. Hippocrates doesn't help a lot here.

In modern times French philosopher René Descartes (1596–1650) became something like the philosophical godfather of the mind-body problem with his approach known as "dualism." Mind and brain are two different substances, he reasoned. The brain is clearly a material organ, the mind, however, is obviously immaterial. The question to be answered would be, what the relationship between these two distinct substances was, how the one could interact with and even control the other.

Descartes was not only a superb philosopher and an outstanding mathematician, who, by the way, invented the Cartesian co-ordinate system, which you may remember and perhaps dread from math class (the name comes from his Latinized name Cartesius). Descartes was also very much interested in anatomy, and it is from his knowledge of the brain that he drew the conclusion that, since the left and right hemisphere of the brain are separate entities connected by the pineal gland, it must be there that the mind and the soul of a person are situated and where the mind kind of "plugs in" into the body and exerts control over it (*Treatise of Man* and *Passions of the Soul*). Needless to say, such a dualism doesn't have a lot of support in the scientific community anymore.

And then there are those philosophers who strongly disagree with the concept of such a dualism in which the mind is a separate entity, supporting a "monism" (Greek "monos" = one, single) of brain and mind instead. In 1874 English biologist Thomas Huxley, for example, quite fervently advocated the idea that mental events are simply caused by physical events in the brain and cannot, in return, have any influence on the body or elsewhere in the physical world. It's the brain that does stuff, the mind only kind of "happens." Like a shadow on the wall that cannot influence the person it accompanies. What we call "the mind" was therefore just an "epiphenomenon", a collateral product of the brain. In this view we are just biological machines ("automata") who think that they think. Not very flattering for our egos, right?

In his 1992 book *The Rediscovery of the Mind* the philosopher John Searle of the University of California, Berkeley, suggested a different solution to the mind-body problem: The mere fact that we use different words to refer to the mind and the brain can lead us into the trap of a false dilemma by either referring to one or the other. In reality, Searle argues, the brain and the mind are more like looking at the same thing from a microscopic and a macroscopic perspective. Individual water molecules aren't "wet", but if you have billions and billions of them, the property "wet" will emerge. And similarly, Searle holds consciousness as the "emergent property" of the different firing patterns of the neural networks in our brain. But before I can continue writing this chapter, I realize that there are some neurons in my brain that are firing a clear GIMME COFFEE signal.

In Pumpkin We Trust—or Not!

Is it just me or do you also see the Great Pumpkin cartoons as a metaphor for disappointment of faith in God? Waiting alone in a pumpkin patch, but God . . . I mean the Great Pumpkin . . . never shows up and all the other people think you're crazy. And the next morning Linus's feeling of being abandoned by God gives him kind of a "spiritual hangover":

CHARLIE BROWN: Did the "Great Pumpkin" bring you lots of nice presents?

LINUS: Oh, shut up!

or

CHARLIE BROWN: Hey, Linus! How many toys did he bring you?!!

LINUS: I was the victim of a false doctrine . . .

What's a bit troubling is the fact that Linus wouldn't even want to know if the Great Pumpkin exists. In *It's the Great Pumpkin, Charlie Brown* (1966) he writes a letter to the Great Pumpkin saying:

Everyone tells me you're a fake, but I believe in you.

P.S. If you really are a fake, don't tell me. I don't want to know.

From a logical perspective Linus's "doctrine" about the consequence of doubting the existence of the Great Pumpkin is a fallacy, a deceptively bad argument; but for Linus it seems to be especially attractive because of its simplicity! Since being able to detect fallacies in other people's argumentation is essential to good reasoning . . . why not spend a thought or two on fallacies and logic?

How can Linus "prove" his doctrine? That's easy: If the Great Pumpkin doesn't show up, his theory is right because his skeptical "if" has insulted the Great Pumpkin and therefore he remains in hiding. If, however, he did show up, it would all the more so prove Linus's theory.

Now let's try and disprove the Great Pumpkin dogma, and it becomes rather apparent that we can't. He makes an unfalsifiable claim. At the most, Linus's critics could argue for the Great Pumpkin's non-existence at a specific place or time, for example here in this pumpkin patch, but general non-existence cannot be proven. An unfalsifiable claim can, however, just for fun be met with another unfalsifiable claim. Lucy—she is mean enough to do that—could say, "No, Linus, I have a better explanation for the Great Pumpkin's absence last night: I've heard that last week he was killed and eaten by the Great-Pumpkin-Eater—high five!" Okay, Lucy wouldn't say "High five", but you know what I mean.

Fallacies Can Make You (Un)Happy

A number of logical fallacies are associated with false cause-effect-relationships. Probably the most frequently discussed one is *post hoc ergo propter hoc* (Latin: after this, therefore because of this). In the above example where Linus broke a taboo by thoughtlessly doubting the Great Pumpkin's existence ("if you exist . . ."), the fallacy consists in the faulty assumption that the Great Pumpkin's absence can only be explained because Linus insulted him before.

Many modern superstitions can be explained by this same simple pattern: One thing happens after another, therefore it was caused by the former. You see a black cat and later something bad happens . . . for many superstitious people the case is clear: the black cat "caused" the mishap.

There are numerous other cases of faulty argumentation and thinking within the *Peanuts* gang, like for example self-deception through *suppressed evidence* about the realistic chances in a one-sided infatuation as between Sally and her "Sweet Babboo," Linus:

> SALLY: See this valentine I made for Linus? On the inside I wrote "To my Sweet Babboo!"
>
> CHARLIE BROWN: He says that he is not your Sweet Babboo!
>
> SALLY: What does he know?

Lucy and Schroeder, Peppermint Patty and Charlie "Chuck" Brown . . . they all close their eyes to an undesirable reality. Charlie Brown does acknowledge that his love for the Little Red-Haired Girl is totally one-sided ("There's nothing like unrequited love to drain all the flavor out of a peanut butter sandwich"), and yet he prefers his state of silently obsessing and suffering to the healthy alternative of finding another girl to love.

When Charlie Brown has one of his dark moments and just remembers everything that did not go well for him, then—presto!—he is trapped in *confirmation bias*, the tendency to look for evidence to support his hypothesis that he is a loser.

Quite frequent also is the so-called *ad hominem* argument (Latin: to or at the person) in which an irrelevant personal attack on the opponent or his situation is used to weaken his position:

> LUCY: You will never get that kite to fly! Why? Because you're Charlie Brown! . . . Look into this mirror, Charlie Brown! This is the face of failure! A classic failure face! (*The Peanuts Movie*, 2015)

No wonder that after multiple repetitions of such ad hominem attacks Charlie Brown has internalized another fallacy: the *self-fulfilling prophecy*, in which his own expectation of not being able to fly a kite will bring exactly that result.

My Anxieties Have Anxieties

> LINUS: Charlie Brown, you're the only person I know that can take a wonderful season like Christmas and turn it into a problem. Maybe Lucy's right. Of all the Charlie Browns in the world, you're the Charlie Browniest. (*A Charlie Brown Christmas*, 1965)

Monica Lammers has outlined how psychologists diagnose Charlie Brown with signs of an avoidant personality disorder: He has very low self-esteem and feels inferior to others; he is preoccupied with his own shortcomings and thus frequently afraid of embarrassing himself in front of others. And although Charlie Brown longs for the feeling of being loved and, above all, having a relationship with that Little Red-Haired Girl, his hypersensitivity to rejection prevents such developments most of the time. Psychologists who come up with that diagnosis then conclude that for a real-life Charlie Brown it would be highly recommendable to undergo treatment, which would employ techniques such as social skills training, group therapy and exposing Charlie to the situations he is scared of to gradually improve his social contacts.

But I doubt that Charlie Brown would really be diagnosed with an avoidant personality disorder. Let's look at some facts that contradict this diagnosis: At the beginning of *The Peanuts Movie* he enthusiastically announces to all the kids that he is going to try to fly a kite, hoping, of course, that the Kite-Eating Tree is sleeping for the winter.

And let's not forget that he is the proud and dedicated manager of his hapless baseball team and far from avoiding the unpleasant YOU-BLOCKHEAD-treatment they give him, when they blame him for yet another lost game. Nor does it look much like avoidant behavior when he stoically stays on the pitcher's mound in the pouring rain, while all his teammates have already gone home. He also tries to sell Christmas wreaths going from door to door. Not very successfully, as we know, but still . . . he does it.

And secondly, even if Charlie Brown had a mild form of avoidant personality disorder—which would not be completely surprising, given all those "You blockhead!" comments—there still would not be any need for an outside therapeutic intervention, since Charlie already has a go-to-guy in matters of counseling: his philosophical friend Linus.

> LINUS: Listen, Charlie Brown. Ignoring what my sister Lucy says has enabled me to make it this far in life. (*The Peanuts Movie*, 2015)

It seems that Charlie Brown has developed his own coping mechanisms to deal with his apparent shortcomings and failures. He isn't a boohoo-nobody-loves-me type of guy who is so caught in self-pity that he has lost touch with reality.

> CHARLIE BROWN: I don't care what Lucy says. I may have had troubles in the past flying a kite. I may never have won a baseball game. But it's not for the lack of trying. (*The Peanuts Movie*, 2015)

That's the spirit! You may suck at something, but, hey, that's no reason not to do it.

Freedom?—Aaugh!!!

To me it looks like we can detect a better explanation for all his anxieties. His condition seems to display features of something that nineteenth-century Danish existentialist Søren Kierkegaard called "angst" (*The Concept of Anxiety*, 1844). "Angst" in this existential sense is quite different from what we usually refer to with words like "worry" or "fear." Fear has a focus, a direction, like for example the fear you may experience when you walk through a dark back alley in a bad part of town. Or the fear of being bitten by the big, aggressively barking dog that is coming towards you. Angst is different. It affects the whole body, the whole person, and most of all it does not have a specific focus.

The French existentialist philosopher Jean-Paul Sartre believes that the only suitable word to describe this state when you realize that you are thrown into your existence and condemned to be free is "nausea" (*Nausea,* 1949). Have you ever wondered why in the world of *Peanuts* we never actually "hear" the voices of grownups? Instead we hear that characteristic "Mwaa mwaa mwaa" of a muted trombone. This is no coincidence.

The *Peanuts* kids seem almost abandoned in their own little world, without the traditional forms of guidance through parents or teachers that pass on values from one generation to another. Instead the kids are "condemned to be free," as Sartre would say. No wonder they develop feelings of anxiety, abandonment, not being loved and valued. Needless to say, the existentialist awareness of such freedom goes along with a corresponding awareness of responsibility. When Charlie Brown appears to be "wishy-washy" to the other *Peanuts*, he may just be caught in a paralyzing loop of constant over-analyzing his situation and other people's motives.

In *The Peanuts Movie* Charlie Brown is teamed up with the Little Red-Haired Girl to do a book report together. And what does he do instead of mentally high-fiving himself ("Charlie Brown, you dog!")? He is worried sick about the potentially devastating long-term effect of this little school project:

CHARLIE BROWN: You've got to help me, Linus! I'm not sure I can handle being partners with the Little Red-Haired Girl! How will I support her? I can't afford a mortgage! What if I'm put into escrow?

LINUS: Charlie Brown, you're the only person I know who can turn a book report into a lifelong commitment.

There's one scene in the 1965 TV special *A Charlie Brown Christmas* which is probably the epitome of such unfocused fear that extends to Charlie's whole existence. It's when he comes to Lucy's psychiatric booth asking for her advice. Charlie explains that he knows he should be happy, but he's not. Lucy responds: "Well, as they say on TV, the mere fact that you realize you need help indicates that you are not too far gone. I think we better pinpoint your fears. If we can find out what you're afraid of, we can label it."

What follows is a list of different phobias together with an explanation of what they are about: from hypengyophobia (fear of responsibility), ailurophobia (fear of cats), climacophobia (fear of climbing), thalassophobia (fear of the sea), to gephyrophobia (fear of bridges).

And since Charlie doesn't give her any indication that they're getting anywhere near the reason for his unhappiness, Lucy broadens the scope of her phobia-labeling:

LUCY: Or maybe you have Pantophobia. Do you think you have Pantophobia?

CHARLIE BROWN: What's Pantophobia?

LUCY: The fear of everything.

CHARLIE BROWN: THAT'S IT!!

Well, now that we know that pantophobia isn't the fear of wearing pants (this sounded a lot funnier this morning in the shower), I still doubt that this term "labels" the state of Charlie's emotions adequately. He doesn't show clear signs of depression, nor does he literally suffer from fear of everything: He loves Snoopy; he loves baseball, even if he constantly loses; he loves flying kites, kicking a football and most of all he loves the Little Red-Haired Girl.

She's Something, I'm Nothing

There are only two tragedies in life: not getting what you want—and getting it.

—OSCAR WILDE

No, Oscar Wilde wasn't talking about Charlie Brown and the Little Red-Haired Girl in *The Peanuts Movie*; he wrote this famous aphorism long before *Peanuts*. But doesn't it perfectly reflect the mixed sentiments shared not only by Charlie Brown himself, but also by many viewers of this latest addition to our *Peanuts* DVD collection?

It's one thing that Charlie Brown finally got to see and—more importantly—talk with the Little Red-Haired Girl, but at the same time "We the People," sorry, we the fans are forced to see and hear her, too. Call me nostalgic, call me Kafkaesque, but do we really want to see Charlie Brown start a normal, healthy relationship with that ominous Little Red-Haired Girl? Do we honestly want over fifty years of pining and unrequited love to end?

My answer is NO! And YES! And it's not because after decades of being a *Peanuts* fan Charlie Brown's wishy-washiness is gradually rubbing off on me. The truth of the matter is rather that Charlie Brown's existential angst leaves him in a state, where it finally doesn't matter anymore if he gets into any sort of relationship with the Little Red-Haired Girl or not. As Charlie says, "I think I'm afraid to be happy, because whenever I get too happy, something bad always happens."

That's true, Charlie Brown, but you know what we grown-ups call this phenomenon? Life!

But sadly, whatever advice I may give you, all you will hear is a muted trombone going "Mwaa mwaa mwaa."

8
For Hume the Ball Tolls!

RICHARD GREENE

It's often said that the definition of insanity is doing the same thing over and over again and expecting different results. This saying is usually attributed to Albert Einstein, although he didn't actually say it. It's fun to think about those people who attribute this quote to Einstein over and over again, expecting that will change the fact that he didn't say it.

Regardless of who said it, it seems right. Not that this is a perfect philosophical definition of insanity, but certainly it appears that folks who do, in fact, do the same thing over and over again while expecting different results must be at least a little nuts. If that's right, then Charlie Brown and the gang really put the *nuts* in *Peanuts*!

Part of the charm and appeal of *Peanuts* is the various characters' repetitive commitments to certain futile behaviors. Year in and year out Linus spends Halloween waiting in a pumpkin patch hoping that the Great Pumpkin will make an appearance. Similarly, his sister, Lucy, spends countless hours leaning on Schroeder's piano, hoping that he will take an interest in her (actually, what she really wants is for them to "get married and have lots of children").

Sally, Charlie Brown's kid sister, follows Linus around in hopes that he will show interest in her (she wants him to be her "Sweet Babboo"). Charlie Brown's baseball team repeatedly takes the field in hopes of winning a game, even though they have never won with Charlie Brown as manager. They did win one game, but on that day Charlie Brown wasn't there!

Charlie Brown attempts to fly his kite, even though that kite-eating tree gets his kite every time (and laughs at him in the process!). The list goes on and on, but there is one instance of this sort of futility that eclipses all the others: Charlie Brown's attempts to kick Lucy's football!

Charlie Brown trying and failing to kick Lucy's football has become a fall tradition. There is a short, four-panel weekday, version and a long, multi-panel, Sunday version of the football gag cartoons. The short version goes as follows. In the first panel, Lucy holds the football with one end touching the ground, and her finger on the other end (as if Charlie Brown were trying to kick a field goal in a football game). Sometimes Lucy tries to sound sweet and sincere by singing his name " ♫ ♫ Charlie Brownnnn ♫ ♫ ."

In the second panel, Lucy baits Charlie Brown with some sort of promise to let him kick it "this time." In the third panel we see Lucy pulling the ball away, as Charlie Brown is prone with his face up, hovering above the ground, and screaming "AAUGH!". In the final panel, we see Charlie lying flat on his back looking dejected and defeated (sometimes there is a caption that reads "Wump!" or "Wham!").

The longer version runs pretty much the same, but includes panels where Lucy offers further assurances that she will not pull the ball away ("Look. We'll shake on it okay? Let's shake on it . . . That proves my sincerity."), and panels in which Charlie Brown convinces himself that this time Lucy is sincere ("What could I do? If someone is willing to shake on something you have to trust her.").

What's going on here? Is Charlie Brown just an idiot or a rube or a dupe? One might be tempted to draw that conclusion. Given the sheer number of times he's fallen for the football gag, it's hard not to conclude that he's some kind of fool. But Charlie Brown is no dummy. Things don't always go his way, but on many occasions he's reasonable, smart, insightful, and wise. This raises the question: can we get Charlie Brown off the hook?

What's So Bad about Falling for the Football Gag?

Before we can address the question of whether we can get Charlie Brown off the hook, it will be useful to find out just what he's on the hook for. The "Einstein" quote about insanity provides a little pithy insight, but no one thinks that Charlie Brown is literally insane. Something appears to be going on with Charlie Brown, but his transgression falls somewhere on the continuum that ranges between blithering idiot and gullible or naïve, but otherwise intelligent, human being. So what exactly is he doing wrong?

Note that his error is one of reasoning. He misjudges Lucy time and time again, but we don't fault people for poor judgment; rather, we fault people for repeatedly poor judgment. Anyone can misjudge somebody (especially when that person is purposely being deceptive—Lucy is not unskilled at the short con). It's not the fact that he misjudges Lucy, it's the fact that he continually misjudges Lucy when he ought not do so that is problematic. So what error in reasoning does he commit? He fails to form a good inductive argument that has presented itself to him.

Inductive arguments come in many forms, but the form that is pertinent for our purposes involves using past events as a guide to future events. If, for example, the sun rises every twenty-four hours for billions of years, then one who properly attends to the matter ought to conclude that the sun will rise tomorrow. If every time a character in *Peanuts* asks a question of an adult, the adult responds "Mwaa mwaa mwaa," one ought to conclude that adults in the world of *Peanuts* always respond by saying "Mwaa mwaa mwaa," or perhaps that on the next occasion an adult is asked a question, he or she will answer "Mwaa mwaa mwaa."

Similarly, if every time Lucy offers to hold the football for Charlie Brown to kick, she pulls it away at the last moment, then Charlie Brown ought to conclude that on this occasion she will pull the ball away. (He should also draw the further inference, that it would be unwise for him to kick the ball on this occasion.) So Charlie Brown is guilty of being a poor inductive reasoner (at least where kites, baeball games, and footballs are concerned).

Maybe You're Not a Blockhead, Charlie Brown!

We have our diagnosis—when it comes to reasoning inductively, Charlie Brown is a blockhead! But there may be extenuating circumstances. When it comes to inductive reasoning, an important caveat is that all pertinent information must be factored in. You're justified in believing that the sun will rise tomorrow, based on the fact that it has happened every twenty-four hours for billions of years, but you would lose your justification for that belief if you had good reason to believe that an evil scientist was going to blow up the Earth later in the day (think Dr. Evil from the *Austin Powers* movie series, or some such).

Similarly, after seeking psychiatric advice from Lucy on several occasions and receiving nothing but really bad advice, you'd be justified in believing that the next bit of advice you get from Lucy will also be bad. But suppose that you just found out that Lucy had recently completed an advanced degree in psychiatry. Under these circumstances, you would lose your justification for your belief that the next bit of psychiatric advice you'll get from Lucy will be lousy. So this raises the question of whether there's any pertinent information that Charlie Brown may be factoring in, which can get him off the hook for being a bad inductive reasoner.

Here, I think, history matters. The first time the football gag appeared in *Peanuts* was in 1951. This time it was Violet, not Lucy, who was holding the football. She pulls the ball away at the last moment, but does so, not to dupe Charlie Brown, but, rather, because she is genuinely afraid that he will kick her hand.

The following year he tries it again with Lucy holding the ball, but she doesn't appear to be trying to trick Charlie Brown, either; rather, she is simply worried that his dirty shoes will get her new football dirty. Later in the same strip (it was a longer Sunday strip), he tells her to hold on tight, and she lets him kick the ball, but she holds it so tight that he just trips over it. To this point, Charlie Brown has not been given reason to think Lucy is trying to trick him, and he has every reason to be optimistic that eventually he will get to kick that ball.

As the series goes on, and Lucy becomes more determined to trick Charlie Brown, she always introduces some new "reason" for Charlie Brown to ignore his prior evidence. She offers "reasons" why this time she is credible (for instance, they shook on it, on another occasion she offers him "one hundred million dollars," and so on). Charlie Brown on many occasions considers the inductive argument, and he does so in the right way. He'll say to himself, "I know that she is going to pull the ball away, but . . ." Where the "but . . ." is always a reason to not draw the appropriate conclusion. So matters are not quite as simple as they were first presented, but should we revise our assessment of Charlie Brown's reasoning abilities? Is Charlie Brown an okay reasoner, after all?

In short, no! Even if Charlie Brown is justified in his reasoning at each turn, there is a second inductive argument—a meta-level argument—that presents itself to him. At some point, Charlie Brown should reason as follows. "Every fall Lucy tries to trick me into trying to kick the football, and she offers a reason why this year will be different, and every fall her reason turns out not to be a real reason, or she is just lying, so I should ignore her reasons, and never believe that she will let me kick the football." For this argument, there are no extenuating circumstances. That is, there is no extra bit of information that renders the past events irrelevant. Charlie Brown is simply failing to accept a perfectly good inductive argument, which has presented itself to him.

Sure Charlie Brown's a Blockhead but He's only Humean

Perhaps the great eighteenth-century Scottish philosopher, David Hume, can be of assistance to good ol' Charlie Brown.

Hume raised a worry that has come to be known as "The Problem of Induction." The short version of The Problem of Induction is that there is no rational support for inductive reasoning, except for another inductive argument. We must argue that inductive reasoning has always worked in the past, so it will probably work in the future. This, of course, is both circular and question-begging. If we offer inductive reasoning in defense of inductive reasoning, then inductive reasoning is not justified. If inductive reasoning is not justified, then, Hume points out, it cannot lead to knowledge. (Hume didn't actually use the word "induction," but philosophers agree that this is what he was talking about.)

How does this get Charlie Brown off the hook? If Hume is right, then we are never justified when we reason inductively. On the face of things, it hardly seems fair to criticize Charlie Brown for failing to engage in some inductive argument or other, if the very practice of reasoning inductively is itself unjustified. To do so would be akin to criticizing someone for failing to consult a soothsayer or heed the warnings of a psychic. So Charlie Brown could respond that he didn't see any good reason to embrace the conclusion of the inductive argument to the effect that he shouldn't try to kick the football, regardless of how all his past attempts have worked out.

While this argumentative move is available to Charlie Brown, it comes at quite a price. Hume's argument isn't just an abstract treatise on a particular kind of reasoning. Hume was interested in determining what justifies our ordinary everyday beliefs. Hume wondered about how we know that our senses are reliable and how we can know that the things that we experience are real.

Consider some things that Charlie Brown takes himself to know. He presumably knows that Linus carries a security blanket everywhere he goes, and that Snoopy is a beagle, and that Lucy has a mean streak, and that Peppermint Patty hangs out with Marci, and that Sally loves Linus, and so on. Hume points out that to know these things requires causal reasoning. We reason causally from our experiences of these things to the existence to the truth of these things. But how do we know about causal reasoning? According to Hume, we know about causal reasoning on the basis of experience—we experience what we take to be causes and effects conjoined, and we form beliefs about causal relationships.

But what does our experience presuppose? We have to assume that nature is uniform (if it is not, my experience of the past won't tell me anything about what will happen in the future), and that the past is a good guide to the future, and since that is a fact about the universe just like the ones mentioned a moment ago, we have to rely on causal reasoning to know it (for example, we reason because past pasts have resembled past futures, that the current past will resemble the current future). There is more to the story, but we have seen enough to bring out the implications of all this. Ultimately, on Hume's view, we fail to have justification for any beliefs about the external world. Hume has given us skepticism!

Bringing it back to Charlie Brown, if he uses Hume as a defense for not engaging in inductive reasoning about whether Lucy will pull the football away at the last minute, he also has to abandon his claims to know that Snoopy is his dog, and that the Little Red-Haired Girl is cute, and that Linus carries a blanket everywhere he goes, and that Lucy is mean, and that Sally is dramatic, and so on. In other words, Hume has argued for a kind of skepticism about the external world, and Charlie Brown doesn't want to be a skeptic. Charlie Brown likes knowing things. He is a student of his world, not a doubter of it.

Moreover, there are some responses that philosophers give to Hume's argument, that would tend to undercut Charlie Brown's employment of it. For example, they might give a pragmatic reply. This involves maintaining that even though induction is not justified, in virtue of the circularity that Hume points out, it's still a good way to reason, since you're more likely to wind up with true beliefs if you reason inductively than if you don't. If this is a good response to Hume's argument, then Charlie Brown is back on the hook.

A second response to the problem of induction comes from Hume himself. Hume was famously interested in the tension between what is rational to believe, on the one hand and what is natural to believe on the other. Sure, says Hume, it is not rational to perform acts of induction, but it is natural to do so. Hume thought that we were constituted in such a way that we couldn't help but form inductive inferences. We respond to stimuli in our environment, and naturally form beliefs about the world.

For example, Charlie Brown sees Linus with his blanket time and time again, and naturally forms the belief that next time he sees Linus, Linus will have his blanket with him. For Hume, this is something that Charlie Brown cannot help but do. Contemporary Humeans take it a step further arguing that we are hard-wired to engage in inductive reasoning (even when we know that we are not justified in doing so). So if this is correct, then Hume's argument only gets Charlie Brown off the hook at the expense of maintaining that there is something defective about the way he is wired. We don't have any reason to conclude that there is something wrong with the way that Charlie Brown is wired! It seems like Hume's considered opinion on induction is not going to get Charlie Brown off the hook, after all.

You're Still a Good Man, Charlie Brown!

So it appears that we aren't going to be able rescue our assessment of Charlie Brown by finding some essential feature of his reasoning (that is, by finding the extenuating circumstance in his particular situation), nor are we going to be able to rescue him by rejecting the practice of induction outright. Maybe Charlie Brown is just a blockhead, after all. Not so fast, there is still one last hope: Charlie Brown himself!

Peanuts is one of the most, if not *the* most, beloved comic strips ever, and Charlie Brown is one of the most beloved characters ever. Most folks see at least a little something of themselves in Charlie Brown. He is kind, determined, and honest (especially with himself), but he is also plagued by insecurities, doubt, and some self-loathing. One of the things that people love most about Charlie Brown is that despite his insecurities and his doubts, he always keeps trying. He keeps flying that kite, even though that darned tree always eats it. He keeps trying to get up his nerve to talk to the Little Red-Haired Girl, even though he always loses his nerve. He keeps trotting his baseball team out on the field, even though they always lose. And most importantly, he keeps trying to kick that football, even though on many occasions, he seems to know in advance that Lucy will pull it out of the way.

It's not that Charlie Brown's reasoning process has failed him—he knows exactly what is going to happen; rather, it is that he's determined to kick that ball. From Charlie Brown's perspective, it is worth it to lose the ball game, and to have the tree eat the kite, and to have Lucy pull the ball away at the last moment, because of how great it would be to actually win a baseball game, or fly a kite, or kick a football!

Charlie doesn't mind ending up on his back every November, because the alternative is worse. The alternative is to give up on the dream of kicking the ball!

In this respect Charlie Brown is not unlike most of us. Why do sports fans spend countless hours rooting for a team that is almost certainly going to fail to win a championship in any given year? Because it's worth it. It's great when they do (fans of the Chicago Cubs are encouraged to skip this section). Why do writers spend hours upon hours writing stuff that will certainly end up in the circular file? Because it's great when they write something they like.

Why do princesses, for that matter, kiss so many frogs? Because it's great when one turns out to be a prince. You get the idea. Charlie Brown knows that the endeavor is worth it, because one day it will pay off. Charlie Brown is not a blockhead after all, he's just determined and patient. He's committed!

On one occasion in 1979 Lucy did let Charlie Brown kick the football. In that particular strip, Charlie was in the hospital and Lucy (who apparently is not as evil as she's cracked up to be) promises him that if he recovers, she will let him

9

I Hate Reasons!

RACHEL ROBISON-GREENE

LUCY: Why don't you ever call me "cutie"?

SCHROEDER: What?

LUCY: Why don't you ever come up to me and say "Hi, cutie!"

SCHROEDER: Because I don't think you're that cute.

LUCY: I hate reasons!

Reasons can be pesky sometimes. If we're being rational, reasons can force us to accept some harsh truths. That is *if* we're being rational. Like the average human being, the characters in the *Peanuts* series are wishy-washy when it comes to their commitment to rationality.

When we read *Peanuts* comic strips or watch *Peanuts* specials, it's easy to forget that the characters are supposed to be in *kindergarten*. Though this fact comes up often in the strip, every time I stumble across it in a panel, I am taken aback. I guess that I tend to think of the characters as fifth- or sixth-graders. Their conversations with each and their observations about the world are too profound to be the musings of five-year-olds. We have all encountered five-year-olds. Even if you aren't inclined to spend much time with kids, you've at least *been* a five-year-old.

Children in kindergarten are just starting to learn their letters and numbers. It is at just this stage that children learn the fundamentals of how to read. They are just learning how to engage the world in such a way that the beliefs that they form will be reliably true. Many of their mistakes can be rather comical. These types of critical thinking errors are on display in *Peanuts*.

We don't hold five-year olds to adult standards. At this stage in their lives, we strive to teach them how to be good friends, students, citizens, reasoners, and hopefully all-around good people. Ideally, we guide young people to be the best versions of themselves both by teaching them standards and principles explicitly and by demonstrating through example.

The *Peanuts* comic strip flips the script. Five-year-olds demonstrate to us, either through their virtues or through their mistakes, how we should strive to live good lives.

A substantial number of *Peanuts* comic strips over the years mirror, in the behavior of five-year olds, the bad critical thinking practices of adults. As readers, we suspend our disbelief about whether kids this young would actually be having conversations about these kinds of things in the first place. More than that, though, casting five-year-olds in the roles of people engaging in adult conversations allows us to criticize and laugh at those practices without becoming defensive of our own practices or putting our peers in the position to feel defensive.

Listening to Lucy's Lectures Always Makes My Stomach Hurt

In your interactions with other people, how often do those people change their beliefs in response to evidence or in response to sound arguments? More importantly, how often do *you* change long-held views of *your own* in light of new evidence or stronger arguments? Hopefully the answer is, "All the time." "Every time."

People tend to be fairly set in their ways and are reluctant to change their beliefs even when the best evidence supports a position that is different from the one that they hold.

People are also often bad at identifying what good evidence even looks like. They often tend to take their own gut intuitions as if they constitute sufficient evidence for the things that they believe. Intuitions aren't always a bad thing, so long as they are *informed* intuitions. Imagine, for example, that you call a car mechanic when your vehicle is acting up. Before scheduling an appointment, the mechanic asks you to describe the problem with your car. Based on what you describe, the mechanic makes a few predictions about what might be wrong with it and gives you ballpark estimates for what it would cost to fix each of the potential problems. The mechanic, at this point, doesn't have enough evidence to definitively determine what has gone wrong with your car. But we're justified in treating his or her intuitions as if they have some credibility because those intuitions are informed.

Consider, however, the case of climate change. Many people have beliefs about the issue that are based on nothing more than their own individual intuition. Some people find it implausible that seemingly innocuous human behaviors could lead to such catastrophic consequences for the planet. Given what's at stake here, this is a very dangerous question to resolve using purely individual intuition alone, if that individual intuition doesn't happen to be the intuition of a climate scientist.

Errors of this type are known as fallacious appeals to authority. We commit this fallacy when we accept (and suggest that others also accept) evidence based on the "expertise" of a person who is not actually an expert on the topic in question. Sometimes, the non-expert to whom the person is fallaciously appealing is himself or herself.

Consider Lucy's actions in a series of comic strips from the years between 1955 and 1957. In the first panel of this particular series, Charlie and Lucy lean against a brick wall. Charlie wonders aloud whether, now that spring has come, the birds will be returning from the south where they flew for the winter. Incredulous, Lucy asks Charlie what he is talking about. Charlie responds, "From the south. Didn't you know that birds fly south for the winter?" Lucy laughs long and hard and says, "In all my life Charlie Brown, I've never met anyone with an imagination like yours!"

In the panels to come, Charlie continues to insist that birds do, indeed, fly south for the winter. Finally, Lucy admits that her schoolteacher confirmed that Charlie was right.

LUCY: I asked my teacher today about this bird business.

CHARLIE: Oh?

LUCY: She said you were right Charlie Brown . . . Some birds do fly south for the winter . . . you know what?

CHARLIE: What?

LUCY: I think I'll see if they'll let me change teachers.

This panel is amusing because Lucy is being irrational. Instead of changing her beliefs in response to good evidence, she decides to seek out an "expert" who will confirm what she already believed—that birds do not fly south for the winter.

We could laugh and forget all about this little strip, except these aren't ordinary five year olds. These are tiny philosophers who, through the disarming device of their childhood, offer lessons that we would do well to take to heart. How many of us engage in this sort of practice ourselves, especially in the age of the Internet? When we encounter a study that goes against a conclusion we have already settled upon, how many of us immediately conclude that there must already be a study, equally as strong, that supports the conclusion to which we were already committed? Charlie Brown and friends challenge us to refine our critical thinking skills.

In another series of strips from 1955 to 1957, Charlie Brown is similarly frustrated by Lucy's reasoning. Lucy and Charlie Brown discuss the topic of the Earth becoming smaller. It's obvious from the context that Charlie means this metaphorically, in the sense that the world (even in the 1950s!) is becoming increasingly globalized (for example it is easier to communicate with others across the globe or reach far-off destinations by airplane). This launches Lucy into utter paranoia. For the next several panels, she admonishes her fellow five-year-olds to stop doing things like walking on the ground rather than the sidewalk, sliding into home base, playing jump rope, etc. She cries out in despair, "You're wearing down the Earth!"

Finally, Charlie, to set Lucy straight and to relieve her suffering, reads to her from a book on the subject.

> CHARLIE: [*reading from the book*] Listen to this Lucy, "The world is getting smaller every day . . . Not that the earth itself is actually shrinking. No, no . . . It is the improvements being made in transportation that are reducing distances from place to place around the globe."

> LUCY: I never noticed it before Charlie Brown . . . but you have a funny nose!

Here again, the critical thinking skills that are brought to bear by Lucy are not overly problematic for a child in kindergarten. But the strip highlights common missteps in the critical thinking practices of adults. We too, often ignore evidence that undermines our views when we're concerned that such evidence will make us appear stupid or silly.

In another series of strips from around the same time, Charlie Brown watches Lucy as she parades Linus around, telling him the name of the various trees in their neighborhood. She doesn't identify any of them correctly, but reports the names to Linus with complete confidence. At one point, she even claims that a neighborhood telephone poll is a tree, specially planted by the telephone company to serve the purposes they need it to serve. Charlie Brown eventually gets fed up.

> LUCY: What do you mean, I make your stomach hurt?

CHARLIE: *You do!* You say stupid things and I get all worked up and my stomach starts to hurt!

LUCY: Just because of what *I* say Charlie Brown?

CHARLIE: Yes!

LUCY: Are you sure it isn't *love*?

Charlie Brown tries to tell Lucy that she's doing something troubling by offering this "information" to Linus without evidence. Instead of considering the criticism being leveled against her, she blames emotion for Charlie Brown's distress.

Linus eventually can't take it anymore. After Lucy reports to him that, though most people believe that leaves fall off of the trees in the autumn, the truth is that they jump off of the trees to escape the squirrels. Linus's stomach also starts to hurt and he joins Charlie on the curb, saying, "That's it! Move over Charlie Brown!"

In the Book of Life, the Answers Aren't in the Back

Linus and Charlie Brown are understandably frustrated with Lucy's behavior. This strip and the others like it highlights a number of important obligations that human beings have to one another. These are obligations that have been recognized by a number of prominent philosophers over the years. Most noteworthy among them are philosophers like Immanuel Kant and William K. Clifford.

The first obligation here is that we shouldn't lie to one another. Human beings are unique in the sense that they have developed advanced capacities to use language. We are social creatures, and part of the reason that we were able to survive as a species is that we are able to communicate and co-ordinate with one another. The ability to co-ordinate requires a trust in one another to tell the truth. Indeed, there would be little reason to use language to communicate with one another if we could never trust each other to tell the truth! Lucy is violating the obligation that she has to the rest of the children.

I Hate Reasons!

Perhaps Lucy isn't trying to lie. Perhaps she genuinely believes that giant oaks, palm trees, bamboo, and telephone-pole trees planted specially by the telephone company, all at once populate her neighborhood. Even so, Lucy is still violating an obligation that she has to the other children. When we say that we have an obligation to others to avoid telling lies, what we typically have in mind is the intentional telling of falsehoods.

We tend to think that lying requires the intent to be deceptive. But our moral responsibilities to one another extend past a mere obligation to refrain from being intentionally deceptive. We also have an obligation to see to it that, when we speak, we say only things that we have good evidence to believe are true. Lucy clearly doesn't have good reason to believe that palm trees and bamboo grow naturally in her neighborhood.

When one person reports beliefs that are based on insufficient evidence to other people, harms go beyond a mere violation of duty. There can also be very negative practical consequences. Consider, for example, the case of people who believe on the basis of insufficient evidence that vaccines cause autism. The consequences of having that belief extend beyond the simple harm involved with having a false belief. If you have the belief, and you encourage other people to have it as well, people stop vaccinating their children and society at large loses its herd immunity to deadly diseases like measles and smallpox.

Some of Lucy's critical thinking missteps could, potentially, have bad consequences. For example, in one strip, Lucy admonishes Schroeder for spending so much time playing the piano.

LUCY: Schroeder, why don't you give up this classical music thing? Don't you know that there are over eighty million piano students in this country? And less than one percent of them ever make a real living at it!

SCHROEDER: Where did you get those figures?

LUCY: I just made them up . . .

As all *Peanuts* fans know, Schroeder has an all-consuming passion to become a composer, following in the footsteps of his idol—Beethoven. That passion represents the most fundamental aspect of his identity. Imagine what would happen to Schroeder if he believed Lucy about his prospects of becoming a professional musician! Schroeder is obviously some kind of musical prodigy—no one can play the piano like that in kindergarten! (In fact, there is good reason to believe that Schroeder is even younger than the rest of the gang. His character is initially introduced in a strip that appeared on May 30th 1951. Schroeder is a baby at the time. Later in the strip, he is presented as if he's the same age as the rest of the characters). Schroeder's prospects as a professional pianist are likely much better than Lucy would have him believe. If he listened to Lucy, his dreams might be dashed. Given all that is at stake, Lucy has a moral responsibility to Linus not to report statistics that she pulls out of the air.

In another strip, Lucy watches with annoyance as Snoopy bounces around happily.

LUCY: You'll be sorry Snoopy! My great-grandmother says if you're too happy today, something bad will happen to you tomorrow!

SNOOPY: [*continues to bounce*]

LUCY: *Are you trying to make a fool out of my great-grandmother?*

This strip exemplifies several common errors in reasoning. Again, she is engaging in a fallacious appeal to authority. Lucy's grandmother isn't an authority on this topic. One or both of two other common fallacies are also being committed.

Perhaps Lucy's grandmother has observed that happy times are often followed by sad times. She concludes, on that basis, that excessively happy times actually *cause* sad times. This is called the False Cause Fallacy. The Latin name for the fallacy is *post hoc ergo propter hoc*, which means "after this therefore because of this." The fact that one event precedes another event in time does not entail that the first event caused the second event.

Lucy's grandmother, and Lucy herself, are also committing a fallacious appeal to superstition. Our happiness on one day, all things being equal, has no impact on whether sad things will happen the next day. Again, though, this is a critical thinking mistake to which human beings are prone. Like all emotions, happiness is fleeting. When things are going well, it is a common experience for people to fear that things are "too good to be true" and that the happiness can't last. It is fallacious to conclude that the happier you are, the more likely it is that sadness will shortly follow.

> You have humility, nobility and a sense of honor that is very rare indeed!

This famous line from *You're a Good Man, Charlie Brown* may describe Charlie, but it certainly doesn't describe Lucy. Lucy is prone to certain types of critical thinking errors for much the same reason that some people we know are prone to the same mistake. She lacks intellectual honesty and humility. That doesn't mean that Lucy isn't smart. She's clearly one of the smartest characters in the strip. The problem is, she wants to know things, but she wants to believe that she knows them *now*. She is, seemingly, embarrassed when she doesn't have all of the answers, even though she's only five!

This is a lesson that we can all afford to learn. Some beliefs require evidence that is more difficult to obtain than others. Not all opinions should be treated equally. In order to identify trees, for example, you must have some background in horticulture. We're not born with those kinds of truths about the world just embedded in our heads. They require hard work and study. That's why Lucy's psychiatric advice is terrible. She doesn't know what she's doing. At the very least, Lucy, and the rest of us, should avoid "self-realizations" like this one:

> **LUCY:** I never made a mistake in my life. I thought I did once, but I was wrong.

10
Does Snoopy Dream of Electric Sheep?

FERNANDO GABRIEL PAGNONI BERNS

This Neighborhood Needs a Normal Dog!

Charlie Brown wants to play a little with his pet dog, Snoopy. The game's easy: throw a baseball far away so Snoopy can chase it. However, Charlie throws it and Snoopy automatically catches it directly behind him. Snoopy sits with the ball in his mouth. The game is ruined since Snoopy had refused to follow the logic behind this pastime. Charlie stomps off saying "What this neighborhood needs is some plain ol' ordinary dogs!" (*Complete Peanuts*, Volume 3, p. 11). Charlie considers Snoopy to be many things, but not normal.

What makes Snoopy a peculiar dog? Why is he not just an ordinary dog? Maybe because this particular dog loves candy? No; many dogs love candy. Because he loves snowflakes? Probably not. Because he's always hungry? Nope. Is it because this dog loves philosophy? Now we're getting close.

What makes Snoopy special as a dog is the fact that this animal can think—and sometimes, act—like a human being. He loves to think about the state of his life while lying on his back on top of his doghouse, looking up into the sky. Great philosophers such as Immanuel Kant get inspiration when looking at the starry sky, so why not Snoopy? Also, this particular dog philosophizes about the state of the entire world and humanity while looking skyward. Furthermore, he behaves like a human being, using an unusual degree of reasoning ability (for a dog, anyway).

Yep, he does that. Sometimes. And yet sometimes, Snoopy behaves just like a plain old dog. He barks, eats, and sleeps, like any normal dog. So, Snoopy's true status is ambiguous. Sometimes he's just a dog and sometimes, he's something more.

Snoopy embodies the slippage between the spheres of the human and the animal, spheres considered as mutually exclusive, according to philosopher Randy Malamud, "with no common ground" (*Poetic Animals and Animal Souls*, p. 67). Snoopy is an interesting case study for the new branch of philosophy known as "animal studies." Animal studies looks at the ways in which we think of animals, including the ways in which popular culture represents—and sometimes misrepresents—animals.

From Brute Machines to Nonhuman Animals

Animals and their relationship with philosophy started on the wrong foot: René Descartes (1596–1650), the father of modern philosophy and the founder of rational method in philosophical thought, called animals "nature's machines." He believed animals were incapable of feeling pain or pleasure.

Descartes argued that the mind or soul is distinct from the body and cannot be described in terms of the physical body, although the mind can affect the body through the exercise of free will. While the body is material, the mind is non-material. Human agency, following Descartes, is not the outcome of physical causes. Humans act in one way rather than another because *they want to.*

This line of thinking raises the question of whether or not animals have something that could be called a "mind" or "soul"—the source of free will in Descartes's reasoning. The answer for Descartes—and much of the philosophy that comes after him—is a simple one. Animals can't have any free will because they are not moral beings with consciousness—they don't possess a mind or soul. They have no sense of morality. Thus they are not beings with a sense of purpose.

As a consequence of this reasoning, animals are not so much beings as they are objects. As objects, they are property belonging to the superior humans. And, as objects or property, they have no rights. Based on this set of assumptions, "animals were considered important only to the extent that they could be exploited to improve the existence of humans" (Annie Potts, "The Mark of the Beast," p. 134). Humans are infinitely superior to animals.

This is an idea that Charlie Brown sometimes embraces with gusto. On occasion, Charlie explicitly states that he, as a human being, is superior to his pet. In fact, he screams that very thing to his very uninterested dog. When Snoopy—tired of hearing Charlie scream at him—attacks his "master," the boy angrily states that his dog has to resort to violence because the animal is losing the discussion (*Complete Peanuts*, Volume 5, p. 20). This way, Charlie frames Snoopy within the "nature's machine" framework. Snoopy is just a brute animal prone to instinctive violence.

Charlie doesn't mention at this point that he has been discussing this matter with a dog and that the dog attacked him only after becoming bored with the discussion. Still, it can be argued that Charlie is a fervent follower of Descartes's philosophy. Reckoning the reasoning powers of a rational soul as exclusively human, it limits all animals to the mechanical programming of instinctual response.

Over the last two decades, however, the humanities have been experiencing a new approach to animals that has "revolutionized humanities and social science disciplines" (*Knowing Animals*, p. 1). The multi-disciplinary field of "animal studies" gives a new license to scholars in the humanities and social sciences to speak with expertise about aspects of the animal world, previously only discussed within disciplines such as biology.

The very idea of us as human beings—how we comprehend and experience ourselves as humans—is closely tied up with our ideas about animals. How? Traditionally, humans have thought of themselves as being contrasted with "nature's machines" that serve us. We are what animals are not: rational beings with a soul.

One sign of the new thinking is the growing popularity of the term "nonhuman animals," instead of simply "animals," acknowledging that humans are part of the animal kingdom. Practitioners of animal studies consider humans as animals amongst other animals. This new terminology tends to blur the allegedly clear boundaries between the human sphere and the animal sphere. Our concepts and behavior are never purely human but owe something to our general animal nature.

You Can't Pin Snoopy Down

The concept of animals that behaved like human beings was not new when *Peanuts* made its debut decades ago. Animals which think and talk like humans have been commonplaces of human culture for thousands of years, in such stories as the temptation of Eve, Balaam's Ass, and Aesop's Fables.

Before Disney, animated cartoons like *Felix the Cat* have always featured talking animals. Disney's Mickey Mouse, who at first looked like an adult ugly rat, rapidly evolved during the 1930s into a more and more anthropomorphic creation. Disney's animals, as they gained popularity, behaved increasingly like humans. Donald Duck even blushes when caught "naked," thus denoting that wardrobe is an important thing for these animals with a sense of fashion and modesty. As Jakob von Uexküll points out, "In Disney cartoons animals must be clothed like humans and talk like humans before we accept them as sufficiently human to take them seriously" (p. 21). The equally popular Warner Brothers' cartoons like Bugs Bunny and Sylvester the Puddy Tat don't wear clothes but do talk like humans. Cartoon audiences can sympathize better with anthropomorphic creatures who handle things the way humans do.

Like Disney's and Warner Brothers' animals, Snoopy gets more human-like as years go by. In this sense, Snoopy is not that different from other cultural representations of animals.

However, unlike Donald Duck or Mickey Mouse, Snoopy constantly slips in and out of his roles as a plain old animal and an almost human animal. Sometimes he's just a dog. And sometimes, he's the smartest of philosophers. He never remains too long in one role. You cannot pin him down.

Snoopy constantly shifts between his role as an animal with anthropomorphic features and his role as just a plain old animal. The different characters address him sometimes as just a dog but on other occasions, as a human-like creature. Snoopy cannot talk, an issue related to animality, but he can think and reason, issues both related to humanity. He is fed by humans just like any other animal, but Snoopy also receives (and reads!) letters from publishers.

When it comes to nonhuman animals, many humans are more comfortable assuming that other species will act in ways that are predictable and mechanistic. However, Snoopy challenges, with his recurrent shifting of categories, the clear-cut notions of animals and nonhuman animals. Moreover, humanity seems to rest only in a series of easily-to-imitate gestures rather than in essential traits, making it difficult to establish firm boundaries.

Snoopy as a Plain Old Dog

Snoopy is often addressed as just a dog, Charlie Brown's pet. Nobody seems to see in him more than what he is: an animal. For example, when Charlie Brown looks desperately for his furry hat, he finds that Snoopy has used it as a soft warm bed (*Complete Peanuts*, Volume 4, p. 21). This action closely follows—as any individual with a dog knows—the common behavior of dogs. They love to sleep in forbidden places. Charlie is touched by the image and leaves his pet alone.

On another occasion, Snoopy steals a hat like any dog might: biting down on it and running away with the trophy in his mouth (*Complete Peanuts*, Volume 5, p. 17). Sometimes, Snoopy looks intently at someone eating, with the hope of getting some food (Volume 4, p. 78). Everyone knows that dogs do that disturbing thing. Further, Snoopy often tries to get Linus's blanket. The dog usually runs up, quickly grabs the blanket in his mouth, and drags Linus along with it. He loves to misbehave, eat, and sleep (sometimes, upon somebody, as many real dogs do in real life).

In all these examples, Snoopy is just a dog and everybody around him addresses him as such. His representation closely follows that of real dogs and the humor of the series comes from an animal behaving no differently from any of the countless Internet videos with cats and dogs doing cute things. In these scenarios, Snoopy is a domesticated nonhuman animal, "created" by humans to be part of society and fulfill needs and desires. There is some "bad" behavior here and there, true. But animal behavioral problems are actually normal and are expected in pets.

However, and even if Snoopy never entirely abandoned his animal behavior, he adopted human qualities through the years. In some occasions, the characters seem to get slightly scared about the permeability of the boundaries between what is human and what animal.

Snoopy, the Thinking Dog

As years go by and Snoopy becomes more intelligent, the characters seem to get more and more determined to put the little dog in his "true" position: that of an animal, thus calming their anxieties about animal expected behavior. There are not that many examples, but from time to time, the human characters around Snoopy try to get the dog to morph back to his former self, that of a plain old dog.

We've seen that Charlie struggled to make Snoopy understand not only that he is just a dog, but that he is not smart enough—not "human" enough. Clearly, Charlie equates intelligence with humanity. On other occasions, Charlie teaches Snoopy how to walk on his hind legs. When the dog learns quickly, Charlie is disgusted (Volume 4, p. 77). Several times, Lucy tries to teach Snoopy dog tricks. Mostly, she does so to put Snoopy within the realm of animality. She tries to teach Snoopy to behave like an animal. "From now on, when

I speak you come crawling!" (Volume 4, p. 113). In the beginning, it seems that Snoopy will obey, but at the last minute, he mocks his "oppressors," and in doing so, he displays human qualities.

Contradictorily, training pets is, in part, a matter of turning them into human-like creatures capable of doing human-like deeds. People enjoy teaching "tricks" to pets and getting them to perform for an audience. This kind of animal-human relationship can be criticized on ethical grounds. Some philosophers maintain that animal training—even for silly tricks—in general "comes to be seen as something that is always an unwarranted and cruel manipulation" of animal beings (Erin McKenna, p. 7).

In *Peanuts*, the main characters fall into contradictions: they want to teach Snoopy tricks—so he can perform for them as an actor—but they chastise him when he turns into a human-like creature. This contradiction is common in real life outside comic strips: people want their pets to behave in more "civilized" ways—if an animal is considered "good" or "cute," it is usually because they have demonstrated some form of human-like behavior—but also want their pets to be objects or property for family fun—beings without agency.

Snoopy himself sometimes legitimizes the hierarchical boundaries between humans and nonhuman animals. When served "dog food," Snoopy thinks that the name sounds "so unappetizing" (*Complete Peanuts*, Volume 4, p. 61). This humorous moment is complex: Snoopy seems to understand that "food for animals" is less tasty, somehow inferior. Thus, the dog recognizes differences and furthermore, hierarchies, between humans and nonhuman animals. This kind of traditional and conservative thinking—thinking that legitimizes differences and hierarchies between humans and nonhuman animals—seems to haunt Snoopy. "I'm less than human" he depressingly concludes (Volume 5, p. 117).

However, that moment offers other possible complementary readings: on the one hand, Snoopy could acknowledge the fact that, in our world, the term "dog" (and, by extension, "animal") means something less than human—less than a being with agency. On this reading, Snoopy is elaborating on the cultural differences put forth by traditional philosophy. On the other hand, all this thinking comes from a dog, thus establishing clearly that he is a thinking dog, thus blurring the supposedly clear hierarchies. Here is a case of a dog thinking—a human trait—about his inferiority as an animal.

Snoopy, Just Another Guy in the Gang

As Snoopy's anthropomorphic features increased with his popularity, his capacity to mock the distinctions between what is human and what is animal increased as well. His animal characteristics constantly changed as he moved from being considered "simply a dog" to being considered one more guy in the *Peanuts'* gang.

Snoopy is still mute, as dogs are, and still sleeps in his doghouse. He's still a dog, which humans must care for. Charlie feeds him every day and cares for him. Snoopy depends on Charlie. Still, Snoopy is a dog who receives, together with his dog food, letters—which he opens and reads. He even feels sad when he doesn't get a love letter (Volume 11, p. 3) and happy when he receives valentines. He writes stories for magazines and fan letters using a typewriter without anybody noticing anything weird is going on. He's the family dog, but he's invited to play baseball with the gang. Snoopy wears a baseball uniform. He even acts as an attorney to Charlie Brown! (Volume 11, p. 286).

Still, there are times when the characters seem to feel threatened by Snoopy's agency. On occasion, a human declares that Snoopy is going too far in his blurring of boundaries. Charlie Brown angrily mentions to Snoopy that the latter has "been acting awfully independent lately. Don't forget that I'm the one who feeds you! I'm the one who takes care of you. Look at me when I'm talking to you!" (Volume 11, p. 23).

So what exactly is Snoopy? Is he still a dog? Has he become a person? Or he is a complex hybrid between these two spheres? What makes Snoopy so interesting is that he offers no answer to these questions, his status is increasingly blurred, thus producing anxieties about his true nature, anxieties voiced by Charlie himself.

Being human sometimes seems to be just a performance of naturalized gestures rather than an "essence," and still worse, these gestures—writing, reading, getting offended or angry—are easily imitated by nonhuman beings. Thus, being human is a matter of performing certain acts, rather than being some kind of superior entity. Snoopy vanquishes humanity in each of his gestures with increasing ease.

Not That Different

When Charlie confronts Snoopy about his increasing sense of agency—agency that clearly scares the boy—what's Snoopy's answer? The dog takes off his collar and gives it to Charlie. This gesture can be read as one of will and independence—the dog refuses to be treated as property.

Snoopy's gestures rupture traditional ideas of what an animal is and what it is not. Human attitudes are adopted by Snoopy, even though he's still a dog. He slips into a human-like behavior in one moment, only to immediately discard it in the next—embracing his animality with gusto. Readers never know which Snoopy they will find. He's a mockery of the traditional divisions between proper humanity and proper animality.

The marks of distinction such as intellect or emotions fail to apply in the world of *Peanuts*, where the main purpose of animal studies finds a perfect arena: humans and animals are not that different.

IV

Footballs, Footballs Everywhere, and Not a Ball to Kick

11
The Sincerity of St. Linus

WM. CURTIS HOLTZEN

Linus cares a great deal about sincerity, no doubt because he believes the Great Pumpkin cares a great deal about sincerity. As Linus says, "He respects sincerity."

No fewer than seven times does Linus mention sincerity and the Great Pumpkin's respect for it. What is most curious though is that Linus never speaks about himself being sincere but only that his pumpkin patch is the most sincere. Now I've carved a good number of jack-o-lanterns in my time and have eaten my share of pumpkin pie, pumpkin scones, pumpkin bread, pumpkin spice lattes, and even pumpkin chips and salsa (I have even seen pumpkin flavored dog treats!) but never once have I thought "this pumpkin is especially sincere" or lamented "that pie was filled with pumpkin hypocrisy"!

If you've never seen *It's the Great Pumpkin, Charlie Brown*, and I find that quite improbable since you're reading this, one storyline focuses on Linus and his deep faith in the Great Pumpkin. According to Linus, each year the Great Pumpkin rises out of the most sincere of pumpkin patches, flies through the air, and gives toys to all the good children of the world. It's rumored that Charles Schulz created the Great Pumpkin as a way to mock people's preoccupation with Santa Claus when our focus should be on Jesus.

Despite being teased by the other children, Linus remains firm in his belief that the Great Pumpkin will come because his patch is the most sincere. Linus even preaches the Great Pumpkin gospel to Sally, who forgoes "tricks or treats" to spend the evening with Linus waiting in that cold dark pumpkin patch. Even when Sally loses her temper, demanding restitution over being cheated out of "tricks or treats," Linus remains faithful, shaken, but faithful.

While Linus speaks about the pumpkin patch being sincere his chief worry, though he never says it this way, is about his own faith being sincere. Sincerity for Linus entails certainty and surety. He must be absolutely certain in his belief that the Great Pumpkin is coming. There is no room for any hint of doubt! It is in this sense that Linus is most mistaken. He is confusing a sincere faith for an unquestioning and indubitable faith. I aim to show that Linus's faith was sincere and that there was no sign of hypocrisy. I even think Linus should be the patron saint of pumpkin patches!

Just Look, Nothing but Sincerity as Far as the Eye Can See

Sincerity is a curious quality and one that philosophers have not spent a great deal of time unpacking. Honestly, I do not know why, it's a super-interesting topic. Or should I have said that I *sincerely* do not know why?

For many, sincerity is basically a kind of honesty. To be sincere you simply need to be honest in what you say. Even most dictionaries list honesty as a synonym for sincerity. But this seems to miss some important differences between the two words. Honesty is a kind of veracity or truthfulness. When you're honest it means your words or intentions match up with reality. (Honesty should be understood to include more than words since you can speak the truth but do so in a way that misleads the hearer to believe those words are false. The words "Oh sure, I *really* hate that dress" might actually correspond to what the speaker believes. But it could be said in such a sarcastic fashion that the hearer believes the words are false.)

A.D.M. Walker observes that sometimes honesty and sincerity can be two ways of suggesting that there is no "discrepancy between a speaker's utterances and his state of mind" ("The Ideal of Sincerity," p. 487). If I'm known for being a prankster and a colleague comes to find all of his books have been turned upside down and asks me if I'm the one who did this. I could say, "Honestly, I did not do that" and that would roughly mean the same as "I am being sincere, I did not mess with your books."

Perhaps one significant difference between honesty and sincerity is that you can be honest in hurtful ways or with destructive words. Claiming to be sincere about such sentiments would be, well, rather odd. A schoolyard bully could say many hurtful and threatening things to another child ("You are the dumbest kid I know" or "I hate you so much") and while those words and sentiments may be honest it would be strange to suggest the bully was being sincere. Again, if the bully states, "I'm going to punch you in the nose" and does punch you, we can naturally say "That bully was honest about his threat." But it seems unnatural to say "that bully was sincere about his threat" ("The Ideal of Sincerity," p. 487).

Sincerity about an immoral or vicious act or attitude may not strike you as that odd. After all it is not totally unusual to hear someone say, as I heard one person quip about a TV preacher found guilty of bilking millions from his viewers, "He's just so sincerely evil." However, while it may seem normal to say a person is sincerely evil it sounds very strange to say someone is "insincerely evil." Would this be a bad or a good thing? Insincerity means one is being inauthentic, fake, or conflicted. So wouldn't that mean that it would be good to be insincerely evil? What would an insincere liar even look like?

In the very first comic strip to feature the Great Pumpkin, Linus and Charlie Brown disagree over the Great Pumpkin's existence. Linus tries to reach a compromise by saying Charlie Brown can believe in Santa Claus and he will continue believing in the Great Pumpkin. The strip ends with Linus saying, "The way I see it, it doesn't matter what you believe just so you're sincere." I think this is Schulz's jab at those who claim the content or truth of a religious belief does not matter as long as the person sincerely believes.

Those critical of such sentiments usually say something like, "Sincerity cannot be the measure of truth because it is possible to be sincerely wrong." While I understand the intent of such a comment their understanding of sincerity is wrong, but not sincerely wrong. Let's turn this around, what would it mean to be insincerely wrong? Isn't this an oxymoron along the lines of "act naturally," "serious fun," or "Dodge Ram"? Linus rightly and most assuredly believes that sincerity is a positive attribute. He constantly praises his pumpkin patch for its sincerity. He argues that sincerity is that quality that the Great Pumpkin respects the most. If sincerity is a virtuous attribute, then it can't be applied to an unethical behavior or sentiment.

One reason why sincerity can only apply to a good or virtuous attribute may be due to its etymological roots. The English word "sincere" comes from the Latin *sincerus* and *sinceritas* which mean "purity." They also have the connotation of "single-mindedness." Purity denotes that something is unalloyed, that is, there is nothing added that should not belong. Water, if it is pure, has not been mixed with toxins, lead, or unnecessary minerals. Pure joy would be unmixed with feelings of sorrow or frustration.

Sincerity then is a purity of virtue or a single-mindedness concerning a favorable emotion. For example, to be sincerely happy for a friend who gets a promotion at work means that my happiness is pure, unmixed with any feelings of resentment. The sincerity is single-minded in that I am not of "two minds"—at one moment feeling proud and at the next jealous. If sincerity only meant purity, Linus could talk about his pumpkin patch being most sincere meaning that it was weed-free or maybe that it had no other fruit sharing the patch like watermelon or zucchini. However, I think it best in this context to think about sincerity as synonymous with single-minded—pure and unmixed. So now we should ask what it means for Linus's faith in the Great

Pumpkin to be sincere. What is it that Linus seems to think would make his faith insincere?

You Don't Believe the Story of the Great Pumpkin?

While *It's the Great Pumpkin, Charlie Brown* never uses the word "faith" explicitly, Linus's story is clearly one of faith. Throughout the *Peanuts* history Linus is the sage offering both philosophical and religious wisdom. In the first *Peanuts* special, *A Charlie Brown Christmas*, Linus is the one who can see past the commercialism of gifts and bright pink aluminum trees. He quotes from the gospel of Luke in order to share the true meaning of Christmas.

In regard to the Great Pumpkin Linus is just as committed. He writes letters to the Great Pumpkin and invites other children to sing "pumpkin carols" with him. I don't think there is any question whether Linus has faith in the Great Pumpkin. The question, however, is: What conception of faith does Linus seem to have and is this conception a helpful one?

There are scores of books and articles on the nature and meaning of faith. Even before Christianity became the official religion of the Roman Empire theologians and philosophers had been pondering what it means to have faith. Works on the nature of faith can take several directions. Theological works tend to focus on the *object* of faith, that is, the what or whom you have faith in. Philosophical inquires often explore how or whether faith is warranted—do you have good reasons for your beliefs and commitment? But even more fundamental are questions about the nature of faith.

What does it mean to have faith? While there are many ways people answer these questions, I think Linus is an example of the most common approach. Linus seems to think that faith is *belief that* the unseen really exists. Ask most people what it means to have faith and they will describe it as a kind of belief, a mental assent that some statement is true (often called "propositional belief"). For Linus, faith would mean that he believes that the Great Pumpkin is real.

Linus has faith, he believes that the Great Pumpkin will rise out of his patch. In short, Linus's faith is one that can be depicted as *belief that* the Great Pumpkin is real. This approach to faith is often labeled as the "belief model" or the "Thomistic-Catholic" view.

To have a propositional belief is to basically affirm that some statement is true. "I drive a red car" is a proposition I believe to be true. The great medieval philosopher and theologian Thomas Aquinas (1225–1274) argued that the objects of faith are the propositions *about* God. To have faith is to believe that certain statements about God are true. For Aquinas, faith fell between opinion (*opinio*) and knowledge (*scientia*) and because both of these concern our relation to particular propositions, so too does faith.

Opinion, for Aquinas, was somewhat different from how we use the word today. We tend to speak of opinions as preferences. "In my opinion, ice cream is better than pie." For Aquinas though, an opinion was a belief not compelled by logic or evidence. To opine is to choose to believe something, it is an act of the will. This may seem like a peculiar use of opinion but what is important is that opinions are beliefs not determined or caused by their object. Opinions can be doubted and one can fear that the opposite may be true.

Knowledge, on the other hand, is when you can't help but "see" that the proposition is true. The one who knows does not *choose* to believe the proposition but is compelled by evidence to believe its truth. The proposition, "The Democrats will win the White House," is an opinion because it dubitable and believed by choice at some level. But the proposition, "The White House is located in Washington D.C." is knowledge because if you know this you can't help but believe it. It is known, by Aquinas's thinking, with a sense of certainty.

So, according to this way of thinking, faith sits between opinion and knowledge because faith, according to Aquinas, has elements of each. Faith, like opinion, is a belief you choose to affirm. This may be why some have faith and others do not, some choose it, some don't. But like knowledge, faith, in order to be faith, holds its beliefs absolutely assuredly.

Faith must consist of beliefs that are, or at least feel, most certain. Furthermore, like knowledge (and thus unlike opinion), faith is indubitable, fearless, and again certain. Lastly, faith is made up of propositions which are mysteries and not provable by either logic or evidence. This is the kind of faith I suggest Linus affirms.

Good Grief, I Said "If." I Meant "When" He Comes! I'm Doomed

Linus's faith as a kind of propositional belief becomes clear when he utters the fateful words "*if* the Great Pumpkin comes." For Linus this meant that his *belief that* the proposition "the Great Pumpkin exists and will rise out of this pumpkin patch" was in doubt. He did not choose to believe the statement was true with total certainty. Furthermore, his belief is tainted by fear—fear that the statement "the Great Pumpkin exists and will rise out of this pumpkin patch" is false.

In the comic strips Linus's belief model is made even clearer by his attempts (and failures) to make himself believe that the Great Pumpkin is real. In one strip, obviously after another Halloween night in which the Great Pumpkin does not arrive, Linus says to the sky, "Goodnight, farewell, until next year." But in the final cell Linus walks away thinking, "Who am I kidding?" His calling out to the sky was an attempt to make himself believe.

Several other strips have Linus explaining his now defunct belief saying, "I thought for *sure* there was a Great Pumpkin," "I *believed* in the Great Pumpkin, I really did," and "I believed with every fiber of my being." In one strip he even writes a book entitled *My Belief Was Rudely Clobbered*. Linus, like many (but not all) who have followed a Thomistic view of faith, judges that his faith has come to an end because he has expressed some doubt.

Linus is questioning whether his faith is any longer authentic, that is, sincere. Linus seems to think that you must either have faith or doubt, but most assuredly you can't have both. Faith is to hold your beliefs with a sense of certainty. Those beliefs must be unwavering and unquestionable. Where there is doubt there is not belief.

Linus repeatedly affirms the sincerity of his pumpkin patch, and clearly this is a metaphor for his own faith in the Great Pumpkin. "I don't see how a pumpkin patch can be more sincere than this one. You can look all around and there's not a sign of hypocrisy." If for Linus, sincerity is certainty then doubt is hypocrisy.

We can conclude that Linus sees his slip about "if," and not "when," the Great Pumpkin comes as a lack of sincerity, that is, an act of hypocrisy. He wanted to believe this, but for whatever reason (and I can think of a few) Linus has doubts. If faith is to believe something willfully, yet certainly, then Linus may have been hypocritical and insincere. But faith may be something quite different than merely belief, and a sincere faith may be much more than belief held without any doubt. I don't think Linus was insincere nor do I think he was hypocritical when he said "if the Great Pumpkin" comes. In fact, it is even possible to have faith without belief and to a certain extent doubt is what makes faith possible.

I'll Sit in That Pumpkin Patch Until the Great Pumpkin Appears

Some philosophers of religion have downplayed the importance of belief in faith. Some, like Daniel Howard-Snyder, have even argued that faith need not demand belief at all. Let's look at how it is possible to have faith without belief.

There's a distinction between *believing*, *not believing*, and *disbelieving*. For example, Charlie Brown is often tempted to believe that Lucy is telling the truth when she says "I'll hold the ball and you come running and kick it." Charlie Brown can *believe* the proposition, that is, mentally assent that those words are true. Charlie Brown can also *disbelieve* that proposition, which is to hold that Lucy's words are not true. Said another way, disbelief here is to believe that "I'll hold the ball and you come running and kick it" is false.

There is another option. Charlie Brown can simply not believe Lucy's words. He can doubt whether they are in fact true but not so much that he disbelieves, that is, believes her words to be false ("Propositional Faith"). The same can apply to Linus. After all the ridicule he has faced from Charlie Brown, Lucy, Snoopy, and even Sally, Linus no longer *believes that* the Great Pumpkin will rise from his pumpkin patch. His cry "O Great Pumpkin, where are you?" reveals that he has surely begun to doubt. Does Linus *disbelieve* these words? Does he now hold the proposition "the Great Pumpkin will rise from my pumpkin patch" to be false? I don't think so.

Linus, by my lights, does not hold the proposition to be true *or* false. He has no belief about the Great Pumpkin rising from his pumpkin patch. He doubts "the Great Pumpkin will rise from my pumpkin patch" is true. But his actions suggest he may doubt "the Great Pumpkin will rise from my pumpkin patch" to be false even more. Additionally, I think it is his doubt in the truth of the proposition combined with his willingness to remain in the pumpkin patch all alone that demonstrates Linus had faith and it was a sincere faith at that.

Like the Thomistic approach, Linus performs an act of the will. He chooses to stay in that patch. But unlike the Thomistic approach I don't think Linus chose to believe some proposition. In fact, sorry Thomas Aquinas, today's philosophers are nearly unanimous that we are simply not free to choose to believe or not believe something at will (this is known as *doxastic involuntarism*).

While it may be possible to choose to believe something given some time and with some work, we plainly can't pick our beliefs here and now. Go ahead, try, cause yourself to believe that you are at this moment waterskiing and not reading a chapter about faith and philosophy. Or maybe we should try something easier, choose to believe that you are reading a cookbook instead of a philosophy book.

Yeah, I didn't think you could do it. What is possible though is to act on a belief that you are in doubt about—a belief that you hope is true. One can choose to act *as if* the proposition is true even if one does not actually believe it. And that is what Linus does. Linus waits in that pumpkin patch, eventually falling asleep, with Lucy finally getting him at four in the morning. Linus no longer believed that the Great Pumpkin was coming. Even if he did have a whisper of belief (whatever that might mean) he was most definitely not certain the Great Pumpkin was coming! It is this doubt, this lack of certainty, which makes Linus's act of waiting in that patch an act of faith.

It may be that not only can you have faith while also being in doubt, but that without doubt faith may not be possible at all. Faith seems to require a certain amount of risk. To act on a belief that requires nothing of an individual would hardly count as faith, even if the person was not certain in the belief. I have heard folks say that they had faith by flicking that light switch because they did not *know*, but did believe, the light would come on. Oh, please! This is more of an assumption than an act of faith for there was no risk involved, no commitment. The amount of risk necessary for an act to be one of faith is debatable, but to act merely on assumption can't be called faith if there is little to gain or lose.

If Charlie Brown chooses to kick that ball despite his (seemingly rational) doubts, then he is taking a risk—and at this point I think Charlie Brown should rightly disbelieve Lucy! Linus demonstrates a commitment to the Great Pumpkin and risks, not just hypothermia, but further scorn from friends and family. Linus shows that faith is not the absence of doubt but action in the face of doubt. Even though the Great Pumpkin never showed up, Linus nonetheless demonstrated genuine faith. But it was only once his certainty was gone that his faith could really be sincere!

I'll Find a Pumpkin Patch that Is Real Sincere

Linus's faith was not actually sincere when he was most certain and sure in his belief that the Great Pumpkin was real and would rise out of his patch. No, as strange as it may sound, his faith was tainted and adulterated by certainty for where there is certainty there is no room for faith. It was when he acted, risked, and committed in the face of real doubts that Linus's faith became sincere. In the end, Linus did have a sincere pumpkin patch, perhaps the most sincere pumpkin patch anyone could ever know.

12
Aaugh! Why Is Being Moral So Hard?

PATRICK CROSKERY

When I was nine years old, Santa gave me my first book of philosophy: *Still More Peanuts Philosophers*. It was a little 4 × 6 boxed set with the collected wisdom of Charlie Brown, Snoopy, Linus, and Lucy.

I didn't know at the time that it was in fact the fourth collection in a series of *Peanuts Philosophers* books (though the title gives a pretty good hint). I still have this collection of books, and reading through them again recently, I see hints of the deepest issues I have explored as a philosopher in my work on moral theories. In particular, Charles Schulz's humor is often based on *failure*—more specifically, the power of some of the humor results from our recognition that we all fail to be ideal moral individuals.

Philosophers have argued for millennia about what the "one true" moral theory is, and are still a long way from a resolution. But there are three main approaches that most people think are good candidates. Morality may be ultimately about happiness, or it may be about responsibility, or it may be about developing good character. In each case the theory starts with an account of human nature—how that theory sees us at the most fundamental level. It turns out that on all three accounts it's easy for us to fall short, and that *Peanuts* can be used to explore some of the most important failures.

To Make Others Happy (August 13th 1961)

When Lucy asks Charlie Brown why we were put here on Earth, he responds "to make others happy." This corresponds quite closely to the first moral theory we will look at, utilitarianism.

According to this theory, at the end of the day, morality is all about happiness. What makes something wrong is that it hurts people (or animals) and what makes something right is that it makes them happier. Of course, lots of things both harm and benefit people, so the theory has to explain how to balance the trade-offs; the typical utilitarian account is that we should maximize overall happiness.

In the *Still More Peanuts Philosophers* book that Santa gave me, Lucy berates Snoopy, telling him that he wouldn't be so happy if he knew about all the troubles in this world [originally Sept. 21, 1965]. This amusing complaint draws our attention to an interesting puzzle for the utilitarian. We can see this puzzle at the very beginning of one of the founding works of utilitarianism, Jeremy Bentham's *Principles of Morals and Legislation*:

> Nature has placed mankind under the governance of two sovereign masters, pain and pleasure. They alone point out what we ought to do and determine what we shall do; the standard of right and wrong, and the chain of causes and effects, are both fastened to their throne. (p. 11)

Commentators have long noted that the "ought" and the "shall" seem to point to different outcomes. Bentham appears to be arguing that we *shall* be motivated by our experience of pleasure and pain to pursue our own individual happiness, but that concern for the pleasure and pain of others means that what we *should* do is pursue the happiness of all. Which is it? Should Snoopy pursue his own happiness or be miserable because of all the unhappiness in the world he is unable to eliminate?

Lucy's own response to Charlie Brown's account of our purpose here on Earth is to notice that she doesn't seem to be making anyone happy, but then to immediately realize that no one is making her happy either. "Somebody's not doing his job" she cries.

A standard response to the puzzle of individual versus collective good is to note that for the most part the person in the best position to do "the job" of making that person happy is the person him or herself. So it turns out that one of our roles in this theory is to lead happy lives. It is here at this very basic level that Schulz finds much of his humor. Like Charlie Brown, we're not particularly good even at the simplest task—leading a happy life.

Thus, we identify with Charlie Brown as he attempts to pursue a happy life and the world itself seems to be aligned against him. Even the most innocent of childhood activities, flying a kite, is a distinctive challenge for Charlie Brown. He doesn't just have trouble flying a kite in the ordinary way—say, facing poor wind conditions. Rather, there is a kite-eating tree that actively consumes his kite. By bringing the hardship to absurd heights, Schulz allows us to laugh at the flat tires on our way to a job interview or the broken air conditioner on the hottest day of the year. We know that the world is not out to get us, but from time to time it seems that way.

In addition to the natural world, the social world also seems to have it in for Charlie Brown. He doesn't simply receive a candy bar he doesn't like for a Halloween treat—he literally receives a rock from every house. Even as a child I wondered a bit about the families that were giving Charlie Brown rocks. Why did they have rocks to give out at all? Why did they single out Charlie Brown? Once again Schulz uses an absurd extremity to make it easier to find humor in our own fraught interactions with society—from the waiter who makes us wait too long to the teacher who doesn't appreciate that our essay obviously deserves an A.

Sometimes people *are* out to get us, of course, and Schulz highlights the humor in that situation as well. We all give in to our faith in others in circumstances when perhaps we should not, but who can match Charlie Brown's faith that *this time* Lucy will not pull the football out at the last minute? After misguidedly relying on the word of an unreliable friend yet again, it is a relief to be able to say "I feel like Charlie Brown with Lucy and the football."

There is one character in *Peanuts* who regularly experiences happiness. Unfortunately for us, that character is not a human being. Snoopy's happy dance demonstrates that a pure form of joy is possible, elegantly expressed with a few deft strokes from Schulz's pen. What is Snoopy's secret?

In the *Still More Peanuts Philosophers* book, Lucy berates Snoopy a second time. This time she's annoyed that he lives without responsibility. Snoopy "replies" that we all have our hang-ups (originally November 22nd 1967). Indeed, a significant source of Charlie Brown's misery results from the heavy burden of his responsibilities. Linus even manages to make him feel bad for throwing a stone into a pond (it took four thousand years to get to shore, after all.) Charlie Brown mournfully responds, "Everything I do makes me feel guilty" (originally January 22nd 1968).

It we take responsibility for the happiness of the whole world, we're overwhelmed. If, on the other hand, we ignore our responsibilities, we aren't fully human. To see more of Schulz's insight into morality, then, we can turn to responsibility, the foundation for the second moral theory.

It's Always Wrong to Lie (February 20th 1967)

When Charlie Brown's sister Sally accidently takes a crayon home from school and breaks it, she's terrified of her teacher's response. Charlie Brown is indifferent to her problem, so she takes matters into her own hands and lies to the teacher. Charlie Brown is shocked, and appeals to the fact that there is an absolute rule against lying.

The moral theory that emphasizes absolute rules is deontology, as famously explained by Immanuel Kant. A utilitarian might argue that a particular lie is justified because it leads to the greater good, while a Kantian will emphasize that we're responsible for our own actions and choices, not the state of the world. As Kant himself puts it:

To be truthful (honest) in all declarations is, therefore, a sacred and unconditionally commanding decree of reason, limited by no ex-pediency. (*Critique of Practical Reason and Other Writings*, p. 348)

Snoopy once again provides a relatively simple illustration of the theory. When Lucy asks him what he has done for mankind, he "replies" that he hasn't bitten anyone on the leg recently (June 30th 1967). He acknowledges that this is "kind of negative," but his response allows us to draw out the contrast between the deontologist and the utilitarian more deeply.

In response to Lucy's question, Snoopy looks at his choices and determines whether or not the *actions* he has taken have been ethical. Choosing to violate someone's rights by biting that person on the leg would be the violation of a negative right. So his action (not biting) fulfills his duty to mankind, according to Kant's account. While Kantian deontologists recognize that we also have a general duty of charity, it is a limited duty and is not as overwhelming as the utilitarian task of maximizing the happiness of everyone.

Once again, it is not the grand implications of the moral theory that attract Schulz's attention, but rather how we fail to fit the model at the most basic level. There is a clever twist in *Peanuts* that has been so influential that we do not fully appreciate how radical it was. *Peanuts* takes place in a world where adults are never seen (and can only say "Mwaa mwaa mwaa") and the children have a peculiar mix of adult and childish traits. This technique has the effect of highlighting how helpless we all feel when faced with the demands of adulthood.

No single item captures this helplessness more than Linus's security blanket. Schulz was proud of the fact that this motif was so powerful that it became a part of the language (*Conversations*, p. 91). In the strip that ran January 21st 1962 he even has Linus cite "the latest scientific reports" that "a blanket is as important to a child as a hobby is to an adult." Thanks to Schulz, we can all spot the security blankets in our own lives that help us cope with our adult responsibilities.

Lucy's psychiatry stand represents the opposite response to those demands—excessive confidence. Note Schulz's audacity in transforming the classic image of a child's first "business," a lemonade stand, into a psychiatrist's booth ("The Doctor is *in*"). Once again we see Schulz's transformative imagination juxtaposing ideas in a manner that opens up new ways to see ourselves and our roles.

Charlie Brown, like many of us, wonders what Lucy's qualifications are. Lucy responds "I know everything" (October 23rd 1967). As Charlie Brown acknowledges, those are pretty good credentials. In the face of our limited capacity for responsibility, we're all a little bit like Lucy, asserting capacities well beyond what we genuinely possess.

Charlie Brown's own response to the challenge is, of course, to be "wishy-washy." Indeed, if he shows enough strength, he aims at some point to be wishy one day and washy the next (December 31st 1965). When we think about it, we can see the source of Charlie Brown's wishy-washiness—how are we supposed to get the balance right between cowering under our security blankets and trumpeting false knowledge from our psychiatry stand? Perhaps we're still under development. In addition to happiness and responsibility, maybe we should pay attention to character formation. Once again, Schulz is ahead of us, leading to the third moral tradition, virtue theory.

All I Wanted to Do Was Be a Hero (May 26th 1960)

Charlie Brown utters these words while lying in the baseline halfway between third and home, having failed in an epic slide while attempting to steal home. In the preceding strips we have watched him hesitate, calling himself a coward, before finally dashing off in his ill-fated attempt. In another series of strips, Charlie Brown tries to build up the nerve to deliver a Valentine's Day card to the Little Red-Haired Girl. He gives up, of course, and puts it in the mailbox (February 11th 1968).

In the one case Charlie Brown acted when he should not have—being foolhardy instead of courageous. In the other case he did not act when he should have—being cowardly. How can he get it right? The influential Greek philosopher Aristotle pointed out that many of our desirable traits, or virtues, are between two vices in just this way.

> For instance, both fear and confidence and appetite and anger and pity and in general pleasure and pain may be felt both too much and too little, and in both cases not well; but to feel them at the right times, with reference to the right objects, towards the right people, with the right motive, and in the right way, is what is both intermediate and best, and this is characteristic of excellence. (*Nicomachean Ethics*, lines 1106b18–23)

According to the virtue theorist, we develop moral character over time. We emulate those who possess a virtue and gradually over time come to possess it ourselves. The challenges associated with this process are a source of humor for Schulz as well.

How do we know who to emulate? Charlie Brown writes a fan newsletter for his baseball hero, Joe Shlabotnik. He notes such accomplishments as "spectacular catches of routine fly balls" and a .143 batting average (March 8th 1970). With heroes like this, perhaps it is no surprise that Charlie Brown does not succeed at baseball. While excellence in baseball is not a moral virtue, we face the same difficulty selecting role models for genuinely moral traits such as compassion or honesty. Or grit.

In one sense, Charlie Brown is himself a good role model for grit. Under the most challenging of circumstances as manager, pitcher, and batter he fights on. A genuine source of our identification with Charlie Brown is not just that we all experience losing, but also that at some level we admire his grit.

But Charlie Brown himself does not recognize this virtue in himself. Rather, he decides that the secret to success is to grit your teeth. He has his entire team grit their teeth as they bat and, sure enough, it works! Until, of course, Charlie

Brown himself gets up to bat with the bases loaded and a chance to win the game and . . . strikes out (July 5th 1965). He has mistaken the external markers of a virtue for the virtue itself.

We can also feel overwhelmed by the sheer number of virtues we have to acquire, each one involving the long slow process of imitation and internalization. Linus asks Lucy what a good brother should be like and gets a very complete answer (January 8th 1964). Kind, considerate, honest, thrifty, sincere, trusting, faithful, courageous, bold, patient, generous. . . . The strip ends with ellipses (and Linus muttering "Good grief!" to himself). As brothers, parents, neighbors, professionals, and citizens, among our many other roles, we face an equally daunting list.

These roles that we fulfill and the virtues that we must aquire are themselves embedded in a larger cultural narrative, In the TV special *A Charlie Brown Christmas,* one of the most influential narratives in Western cultures, Christianity and the meaning of Christmas are explored with striking subtlety. Schulz examines the error of mistaking flash for substance both with the shiny aluminum trees and Snoopy's prize-winning dog house decorations. He brings out the importance of community as the entire crew ultimately gathers around the bedraggled tree Charlie Brown has selected. In a surprisingly delicate moment he has Linus quote from Luke 8–14 on the birth of Christ and the true meaning of Christmas.

Schulz also uses Linus to bring out the complexity of understanding cultural narratives, through Linus's unyielding commitment to the Great Pumpkin. The very sincerity and humility that made Linus's reading of Luke so powerful make his unending belief in the Great Pumpkin even more sympathetic and amusing. The Great Pumpkin started with Schulz imagining a child jumping the gun on Christmas, but it took on a life of its own, I suspect because it captures the uncertainty we each feel about our particular spiritual beliefs.

Happiness Is a Warm Puppy

At the most basic level, then, we do not seem all that well-suited to any of the moral theories. We're not particularly good at achieving happiness even for ourselves, not to mention making everyone else happy. We're often overwhelmed by our responsibilities and respond by retreating to our security blankets or jumping to wildly excessive over-confidence. We struggle to find role models for the development of our virtues and face a daunting list of further virtues to develop.

The *Peanuts* characters let us laugh a bit at these limitations and realize that at least we aren't as bad off as Charlie Brown. At a deeper level, there is a spirit of hope in *Peanuts* as well. Happiness is, after all, a warm puppy—the simple sense of connection to others is available to us every day if we pay attention.

We may still clutch our security blankets, but we're still able to live up to our responsibilities. The grit that Charlie Brown shows is genuine, and we too have many unrecognized virtues.

Perhaps the humor in *Peanuts* is about failure, but it is a failure that reminds us of success.

13
Linus's Wager

JEFF CERVANTEZ

Linus famously remarked that "There are three things I have learned never to discuss with people: religion, politics, and the Great Pumpkin." Sorry, Linus. We must break with your timeless wisdom to discuss both religion and the Great Pumpkin.

Perhaps, one of the oldest philosophical questions (if not also the most important) concerns the matter of God's existence. Let's assume the evidence for God's existence is ambiguous. Suppose there's a roughly fifty percent probability that God exists. What should we do? Should we wager on God's existence? Or, should we bet against God? This raises an interesting question: Is it always irrational (or even immoral) to hold a belief in the absence of sufficient evidence? Linus would say, No.

The Great Pumpkin and Linus's Wager

The well-known *Peanuts* special *It's the Great Pumpkin, Charlie Brown* (1966) focuses on Linus's belief in The Great Pumpkin. In the absence of sufficient evidence, Linus wagers that the Great Pumpkin exists.

As you might recall, the Great Pumpkin is a mysterious holiday personality (similar to Santa Claus). Linus has great faith in this figure. So much so that each year he forgoes trick or treating to sit in a pumpkin patch on Halloween night. Why? Because Linus bets that when the Great Pumpkin appears those who have believed in him will be better off than those who haven't. Linus insists that when the Great Pumpkin finally appears he will rise out of the pumpkin patch and fly through the air with his bag of toys giving gifts to those children who have believed in him.

Throughout the cartoon special, Linus repeatedly endures mockery and ridicule on account of this faith in the Great Pumpkin. On one occasion, his sister Lucy finds him writing a letter to the Great Pumpkin and tells him "Not again. Writing a letter to a stupid pumpkin? You make me the laughing stock of the neighborhood. All they talk about is my little brother who always writes to the Great Pumpkin. You better cut it out right now or I'll pound you." Linus's faith never falters. He maintains his confidence. He chooses to believe, even in the absence of sufficient evidence, that the Great Pumpkin will rise out of the pumpkin patch on Halloween night.

Unfortunately for Linus, the Great Pumpkin never turns up. Although, humiliated he is nevertheless, unrelenting in his faith. In fact, on the morning after Halloween we find Charlie Brown and Linus talking about The Great Pumpkin's failure to appear.

CHARLIE BROWN: The Great Pumpkin never showed up?

LINUS: Nope.

CHARLIE BROWN: Don't take it too hard, Linus. I've done a lot of stupid things in my life too.

LINUS: Stupid? What do you mean, stupid? Just wait till next year, Charlie Brown. You'll see, next year at this same time. I'll find a pumpkin patch that is real sincere and I'll sit in that pumpkin patch until the Great Pumpkin appears. He'll rise out of that pumpkin patch and he'll fly through the air with his bag of toys. The Great Pumpkin will appear and I'll be waiting for him . . .

Unmoved in his belief in the Great Pumpkin, Linus vows to wait for him again the following Halloween. Is it always irrational (or even immoral) to hold a belief in the absence of sufficient evidence? Although, Linus says, no, William Kingdon Clifford disagrees.

Clifford's Ethics of Belief

In his well-known essay, *The Ethics of Belief*, Clifford argues for a particular standard of belief.

> Clifford's Standard of Belief: It is wrong always, everywhere, and for anyone, to believe anything upon insufficient evidence.

How does Clifford arrive at this standard of belief?

Clifford offers a famous analogy. Consider a ship-owner, he says, one who is about to set sail on a long journey. The ship-owner, however, doubts whether his craft is seaworthy. In fact, he knows that the ship needs many repairs. The ship-owner thinks that before the journey he must have the vessel overhauled and restored to proper working condition. Nevertheless, he decides against doing the needed repairs on account of the great expense it is sure to cost. He manages to convince himself by wishful thinking not to doubt that his ship is ready to sail. So, he turns a blind eye to the evidence and only trusts in providence, believing that the ship will safely make it home. Every time the ship-owner begins to question the seaworthiness of his vessel, he dismisses such thoughts from his mind, believing the ship is fine.

Eventually, the ship-owner begins to believe himself. His belief grows sincere and he is comfortable with his unfounded conviction. On the day the vessel is set to depart, the ship-owner watches the boat exit the bay with a light heart and in good spirit. However, the ship never makes it to her destination. She sinks in the middle of the ocean, killing the crew and passengers.

Clifford asks us to reflect on the moral status of the ship-owner. He contends, and I think rightly so, that the ship-owner is responsible for the death of all those on board. This is true, notwithstanding his sincere belief in the soundness of his vessel. Clifford insists that "the sincerity of his conviction can in no wise help him, because he had no right to believe" that the ship was seaworthy on account of the evidence that was before him. Quite simply, the ship-owner did not acquire his belief by honestly earning it through patient investigation but by dishonestly suppressing his doubts.

Even supposing that the ship was able to successfully complete its voyage, the ship-owner would still be guilty of a serious moral failing. Why? He put the ship's crew and passengers in severe danger without sufficient reason to believe that the ship could complete its journey. Again, the point Clifford is trying to make is it that it is always wrong to accept an idea or belief without sufficient evidence.

We could find comparisons between the ship-owner's faith in his vessel and Linus's belief in the Great Pumpkin. Both focus on the sincerity of their belief as opposed to its accuracy. Both hold belief's that are largely unsubstantiated. Both make important decisions based on a wager. Each bets on what they hope to be true rather than what they have reason to think is true. According to Clifford's view, therefore, they are not entitled to such beliefs. According to Clifford's standard of belief, even as the the ship-owner's faith in the seaworthiness of his vessel is entirely out of place, so too Linus's faith in the Great Pumpkin is far out of bounds and, perhaps, even dangerous to others.

Pascal's Wager

The case Clifford provides is a compelling one. His main target is clearly a certain kind of religious belief motivated by an unjustified wager. The seventeenth-century French philosopher and mathematician, Blaise Pascal offered an alternative rationale for religious belief based on a cost-benefit analysis. This analysis has since been famously dubbed "Pascal's Wager." The idea behind Pascal's wager is the following standard of belief:

Pascal's Standard of Belief: faith is sometimes a logical bet.

Pascal applies his standard of belief to the question of whether we should believe in God. According to Pascal, it's entirely reasonable to believe in God whether or not we have good evidence for doing so.

According to Pascal, we are all compelled to wager one way or the other. Either God (or the Great Pumpkin) exists or he does not. If we choose to believe in God and he exists, then according to Pascal, we win infinite benefits and blessings from God for believing. If we choose to believe in God but it turns out that he does not exist, well, we lose nothing. However, if we choose to not believe in God and in the end we find out that he does exist, then we lose everything. So, according to Pascal, the most logical thing to do is gamble on God.

Clifford is obviously opposed to betting on beliefs. For him, beliefs involve ethical principles and moral duties. We have no moral right to a belief that there is no evidence for. No matter how much we want to believe something, we must only believe based on sufficient reason. Of course, this implies that faith generated belief in God (and belief in the Great Pumpkin) are improper.

Nevertheless, Linus would certainly agree with Pascal's standard of belief (faith is sometimes a logical bet). For Linus, it's reasonable to bet on the Great Pumpkin because for him the benefits of doing so far outweigh the alternatives. As he repeatable proclaims throughout the Halloween special, the Great Pumpkin's gifts and blessings bestowed on the sincere believer are far more desirable than trick or treating.

At one point in *It's the Great Pumpkin, Charlie Brown*, Linus's sister Lucy begins to mock him for his belief. Sally, with her eternal crush on Linus, comes to his defense proclaiming, "You think you're so smart. Just wait until The Great Pumpkin comes. He'll be here. You can bet on that. Linus knows what he's talking about. Linus knows what he's doing." Well, Sally's clearly right about one thing. Lucy certainly thinks she's "so smart." But should we "bet on" The Great Pumpkin? That's another matter entirely.

The whole idea behind Pascal's wager seems disingenuous. The motive is completely misguided. Like the Great Pumpkin, God surely desires people to believe in him, but unlike the Great Pumpkin, not because of the benefits. Rather, God longs for genuine relationships with people based on love. So much for Pascal. But does this mean that Clifford's standard of belief is correct?

The most pressing concern regarding Pascal's wager is the fact that we can't *make* ourselves believe anything. Consider the belief that "the Great Pumpkin exists." Suppose, that if you could sincerely believe that the Great Pumpkin exists you would receive a million-dollar reward. Could you make yourself sincerely believe in the Great Pumpkin, even for such a reward? I doubt it. Sincere beliefs are usually not formed by making ourselves accept them. Sincere beliefs are formed through a process of investigation and reflection.

Clifford's analysis assumes that people have voluntary control of their beliefs (what philosophers call doxastic voluntarism). But there are problems with holding that any such control is possible. We do not always willingly decide what to believe. There is more to believing than making a logical bet (Pascal) and following the evidence (Clifford).

If this is correct, then it's not obvious that Linus must only accept a belief he has hard evidence for. Nevertheless, in case the reader is unconvinced let me introduce William James into the discussion.

William James Comes to Linus's Defense

In spite of the lack of evidence for the Great Pumpkin, could Linus still be justified in believing? Can Linus be rationally (and morally) entitled to such a belief? In his celebrated lecture, "The Will to Believe," William James considers the things we have a right to believe. In his attempt to counter Clifford's standard of belief, James argues that it is sometimes reasonable to choose the better story even without sufficient evidence. According to James, it can be morally appropriate and even intellectually reasonable to choose to believe.

A decision is a choice between competing options. Suppose we're trying to decide between two hypotheses: God exists or he does not. According to James, when we are faced with two competing alternatives we must begin by asking ourselves three questions. First, are the possibilities "living options" for me? Not all alternatives are live options for us, some are dead options.

In my world, the option between believing in the Great Pumpkin or not isn't live. (In the world of *Peanuts*, perhaps it is, at least, it is for Linus.) Though belief in the Great Pumpkin is theoretically a real choice for me since I could accept such a belief if wanted, I have ruled out this option as a live one. On the other hand, choosing between watching *It's the Great Pumpkin, Charlie Brown* or *A Charlie Brown Christmas* is a live option for me. So, James's first criteria is that a choice must be a genuine option for you.

Another question we must ask is whether the decision between competing options is "forced or avoidable?" Clearly, deciding between watching *It's the Great Pumpkin, Charlie Brown* or *A Charlie Brown Christmas* is an avoidable choice. Nothing necessitates my deciding between these two options. I could just as easily choose to watch nothing, or to watch *A Charlie Brown Thanksgiving* instead. Another way to put this is that deciding between these options is not forced. The question of whether we should believe that God exists, however, is forced. We cannot avoid this question. Thus, everyone must make a choice on the matter. Either we believe or we do not.

Finally, according to James, we must ask whether the options represent a "momentous or trivial" decision? A decision between favoring Snoopy or Woodstock is obviously a momentous one. No, no, no, it's not. I'm only kidding. As much as I like Snoopy, this is only a trivial decision. There's nothing significant hanging on the option between favoring Snoopy or Woodstock. This is a very low-stakes decision. The outcome of the choice has little bearing on my life. On the other hand, the choice between making a career change or not is a momentous decision. The outcome is significant.

Is Linus justified in believing in the Great Pumpkin? On Clifford's analysis he is not. Contrary to Clifford however, Linus could be morally justified in forming his belief on the basis of insufficient evidence. According to James, Linus would be justified in doing so when three conditions are met.

When to Believe without Sufficient Evidence

Going with James's argument, for it to be okay for Linus to believe in the Great Pumpkin without compelling evidence requires that the choice between believing in the Great Pumpkin or not must represent an option that is living, forced and momentous. Let's assume Linus's decision meets these conditions. But according to James it must also be the case that there is not decisive evidence against the belief in question (the belief that the Great Pumpkin exists).

If Linus believed that there was, in fact, sufficient evidence for the Great Pumpkin's existence, then by all means, he should accept the belief. However, it doesn't look as if Linus has sufficient evidence. Nevertheless, it also doesn't look as if Linus has decisive evidence for the proposition that the Great Pumpkin *doesn't* exist. In other words, there is insufficient evidence for the belief that there is no Great Pumpkin. So, even without sufficient evidence for the proposition the Great Pumpkin exists, Linus may still be morally justified in this belief.

Suppose that the evidence for the Great Pumpkin is inconclusive. Also, assume that Linus has examined the evidence, reflected on the issues, thought about the problems and still, he is unsure about where the evidence points. It's a fifty-fifty shot whether the Great Pumpkin exists. The evidence could go either way. It is here that Linus's leap of faith is justified. Following James (and the religious thinker Søren Kierkegaard), Linus is morally justified in believing in the Great Pumpkin under these conditions.

Notice that William James does not permit just *any* leap of faith. If Linus's understanding of the evidence were such that he could not, in good faith, believe, then his belief in the Great Pumpkin would be unwarranted. He should not believe. Why? Because in such a case Linus would be no better than Clifford's ship-owner. Belief is not mere wishful thinking. On the contrary, belief is making an informed decision to believe one way rather than the other when the evidence is indeterminate. This is to say, belief can be morally justified even in cases where there is insufficient evidence.

According to James, when confronted with a live option that is also forced and momentous we are morally justified in believing the better story. Not always, but in those situations where our intellect cannot resolve the issue, when we have done our due diligence and are still perplexed, then we are morally justified in believing. We are justified in having faith.

But even if Linus has the right to believe in the Great Pumpkin, why should he choose to believe? The answer is that the belief in question represents the better story.

When life would be greatly impoverished by limiting our beliefs to only what we had sufficient evidence to accept, then we are justified in believing the better story. To illustrate, consider the case of love. I doubt that many people have "sufficient evidence" for falling in love. In fact, perhaps I can be so bold as to say that nobody ought to think that love is formed on the basis on propositional belief. Instead, love is better thought of as an emotion or an attitude that justifies a belief or action. This is true notwithstanding the fact that many relationships, based on love, end—and some end badly.

A lot of failed relationships cause great heartache, great loss of resources and prove to be a waste of time. Nevertheless, few would say in the face of these facts that we should fail to believe in love. Why? Because without love, life would be greatly impoverished. In short, love is worth the risk. This is true though love is uncertain; though we lack sufficient evidence to love; though others choose not to love; though we could be wrong about loving.

The point is: if we waited to love until we were sure about the outcome, then we would be probably never choose to love.

If we limited our love only to cases were we have sufficient evidence for doing so, then our life would be so much the worse. Therefore, our decision to love must, at times, be based on insufficient (propositional) evidence and yet, contra Clifford, it is still arguably morally justified. At the very least, life would be greatly impoverished without love.

Perhaps, Linus could contend that the same is true with respect to believing in the Great Pumpkin. Even as love is sometimes morally justified without sufficient evidence so also faith can be as well. For Linus, believing in the Great Pumpkin makes his life better. It gives him hope, teaches him patience, endurance, grit, and delayed gratification.

Linus's belief in the Great Pumpkin doesn't harm anyone. Sure, he doesn't have sufficient evidence for his belief in the Great Pumpkin, but he also doesn't have sufficient evidence against such a belief either. And, if we accept that Linus's life is greatly impoverished without this belief (as the Halloween special seems to suggest), then believing in the Great Pumpkin is a better story. Consequently, if Linus has done his due diligence, then he's morally justified in maintaining his belief in the Great Pumpkin.

Sometimes, practical considerations force us to make decisions without full knowledge. We must sometimes have faith or else miss out on something potentially significant in our lives. In such cases, we must live by faith or cease to live at all.

Linus, we'll see you in the pumpkin patch next year!

14
Is Lucy a Kantian or Just Mean and Nasty?

CHELSI BARNARD ARCHIBALD

Lucy van Pelt is commonly thought of by *Peanuts* fans as the bossy, opinionated, bully whose assertive nature and blunt truth-telling are often the crux of keeping other characters in check.

Her nature is bold and aggressive. She tells the truth, even when other characters in the series do not want to hear it. She's often portrayed as the villain. She also seems pretty vain. Can we save Lucy from these criticisms? Let's look at her through another lens. Perhaps Lucy is just motivated by a sense of duty.

Does our assessment of Lucy's character change if we understand her as an obsessive rule-follower, someone who believes that there is an objective, universal answer to questions of right and wrong?

The Good Grief and the Categorical Imperative

Any discussion of rule following would be incomplete without a discussion of the thinking of the consummate advocate of rule following—Immanuel Kant. Kant was a German philosopher who argued that reason is the source of morality. Our capacity for reason, then, is where all of the moral rules that we're bound to follow come from.

In any given case, says Kant, to determine whether or not we are satisfying the demands of our duty, we have to determine whether the action we want to perform is universalizable—whether it would be rational for us to will that everyone under the same circumstances did the exact same thing. If it would not be rational for us to desire that everyone act in the way that we are planning on acting, then we're making an exception of ourselves—we're behaving as if the rules that bind the behavior of everyone else are not applicable to us. That's morally wrong. So, according to Kant, it's our intentions that matter in the determination of whether our actions are morally right or morally wrong.

Let's see how this would work in practice. Imagine that Charlie Brown is trying to decide whether he should write the book report that he has been assigned for school. He really doesn't feel like doing it. To decide whether skipping the homework assignment would be morally acceptable, Charlie Brown would have to consider what would happen if everyone, in circumstances like his, skipped out on writing the book report. The result would be that school wouldn't function in the way that it's supposed to, and students wouldn't learn. The whole world would be worse off if no one learned what they were supposed to learn in grade school. This universalization process generates a moral rule—you ought to do your homework. Barring extraordinary circumstances, this is a universal principle that applies to everyone.

If we want to know whether our actions are ethical in a Kantian framework, there is a quick test that we can perform. The first step is to formulate want Kant calls our "maxim." A "maxim" is a reason for action. Let's test one out. Imagine that Lucy constructs the maxim, "In order to get Schroeder to pay some attention to me, I will throw his piano into the Kite-Eating Tree."

The second step, as we've seen, is to universalize our maxim—we must imagine a world in which everyone in circumstances like the ones that we find ourselves in did the thing that we're planning on doing. So let's imagine that everyone who resented something threw that something into a tree from whence it was certain to never return. The next step is to look at the likely outcome. This involves checking for what Kant calls "contradictions."

Contradictions can be of two types: contradictions in conception and contradictions in will. A contradiction in conception happens when your maxim, when universalized, no longer works as a way of satisfying your goal. We have to determine whether, if everyone threw things that frustrated them into the Kite-Eating Tree, it would still be an effective way of getting rid of items. This case is, of course, a little tricky because there is much we don't know about the metaphysics (or even the physics) of Kite-Eating Trees.

Do Kite-Eating Trees have bottomless stomachs? It seems like there is only so much space for kites and pianos to occupy, even in a supernaturally evil tree. It's this concern that motivates many environmentalists to write about what they call "the tragedy of the commons." The idea here is that our collective sense of ownership in the environment isn't met with a corresponding sense of responsibility to protect it.

Charlie Brown can't help it that *his* kite keeps getting stuck in the tree. The tree is a malevolent force in his life. But when Lucy threw Schroeder's piano into the tree, that was certainly done of her own free will. Lucy is making an exception of herself here. If everyone disposed of their problems in shrubbery, it would quickly be the case that it would no longer be possible to do so. There simply isn't enough room. To do so would generate a contradiction in conception, and, as a result, the action is morally wrong.

The second kind of contradiction that Kant mentions is a contradiction in will. You've got a contradiction in will on your hands when no rational person would want to live in a world in which everyone behaved in the way that you're proposing. Kant uses, as an example, the responsibility to help others. Suppose that you're in a situation where you're going about your day, minding your own business, when you come across a child drowning in a lake. You are on vacation, and you had less harrowing plans for your day than engaging in heroics. You construct the maxim. "In order to pursue my own ends, I will refrain from helping others."

Now imagine what would happen if everyone in similar circumstances behaved in that way. What this amounts to is imagining what would happen if no one ever helped another person. The resultant world would be one in which no rational person could will to live. We all need help at some point in our lives. In fact, none of us would survive our own infancy if we couldn't count on the help of others. We are, then, morally obligated to help others when it is called for by the circumstances.

This test will allow us to see whether our intention is really to do our duty in any particular case that we may face. Now that we've got all of that on the table, let's see if Lucy really counts as a Kantian, or if she's just a mean and nasty person.

A Promise Is a Promise

Lucy appears to act in a way that lines up with Kantian philosophy when the *Peanuts* group puts on the Christmas play in *A Charlie Brown Christmas*. Charlie Brown is chosen as the director (It's astounding that Charlie Brown is so frequently cast as a leader when all of his peers view him as wishy-washy). While the other characters are naturally distracted and many are unsure of what their responsibilities are, Lucy points out that it is the duty of the cast members to follow the instructions of the director.

> LUCY: No, no, no! Listen all of you, you've got to take direction! You've got to have discipline. You've got to have respect for your director!

Lucy tends to disregard the feelings, impulses, or personal problems of her friends. As a result, we might be inclined to think that she is a mean, nasty person. But perhaps this isn't true. Perhaps her behavior can be explained by the fact that she considers respect for duty as the most important ethical value.

Let's consider her behavior toward her brother, Linus. She is especially known for being very hard on him. Although he is capable and intelligent, his blue security blanket is a crutch. So, too, is his propensity to suck his thumb. Even though Linus is still very young, plenty of people believe it's time for him to be rid of the blanket. Lucy and her grand-mother dedicate much attention to ridding him of it.

You might think that this behavior is cruel. Lucy, how-ever, believes that she's doing her brother a favor—helping him to satisfy his moral duty to self improvement. She is rid-ding him of his weakness, which she thinks, if left unad-dressed, will be harmful both to Linus and to the group as a whole in the long run.

At one point, Linus runs for president of his class, but his ridiculous belief in the Great Pumpkin and his constant need to carry his blanket and suck his thumb ensures that he loses the election. Lucy tries everything she can think of. She buries the blanket, hides it in a closet for two weeks, and takes it away from Linus "to be washed."

In the November 18th 1971 panel, Lucy sits in her psychi-atric booth, consoling Charlie Brown. He is disappointed in himself because he enabled Linus's dependence on the blan-ket. Linus had, temporarily, triumphed over the dependence, but Charlie Brown felt badly for him and told him that, in his opinion, the habit didn't seem harmful. Lucy corrects Charlie about the sabotage of Linus's developmental step forward.

> **Lucy:** In all of mankind's history, there has never been more dam-age done than by people who thought they were doing the right thing.

Charlie Brown has gone wrong here by assuming that Linus's own sensations of comfort are, by themselves, enough to justify encouraging him to keep his blanket. He is not alone in the belief that such considerations make a moral difference. Some moral philosophers, such as John Stuart Mill and Jeremy Bentham, think that the consequences that follow from an action are the things that make that action either morally right or morally wrong. In particular, the happiness that Linus feels when he holds is security blanket might, all things being equal, make keeping the blanket the right thing to do.

Kant argues that the consequences of an action *cannot* be used to determine if a person has acted morally. The reason is that the consequences could be merely accidental. For example, one of the neighborhood kids might make Charlie Brown feel important (or at least, less invisible) by talking to him, when they were *intending* to insult him instead. Another child might strengthen Linus's faith in the sincerity of his pumpkin patch when their intention was really to make fun of it. The theory of morality that maintains that morality is determined by the consequences of actions can't explain why *these* actions, though they might have good consequences, are actually *bad* actions.

An adequate moral theory needs to capture the fact that the children involved in our examples *intended* to be cruel. For this reason, neither overall levels of comfort nor overall levels of pleasure determine the moral status of an action. Kant thinks that the only way to capture what we want to capture in these kinds of cases is to look at whether the person is acting out of respect for what they have determined to be their duty.

Why does it matter? Why would anyone think that Linus's dependence on his security blanket has any moral significance at all? Kant argues that human beings have a moral responsibility to self-improvement. Consider, for a moment, what would happen if no one ever tried to overcome their challenges. Human beings were able to advance to where they are now in terms of culture, technological advancement, and knowledge of the external world, in no small part because they were able to overcome their weaknesses and develop their strengths.

We cannot rationally will to live in a world in which no one ever tries to overcome their weaknesses. Since we can't universalize that action, it's wrong to encourage Linus to remain tethered to his security blanket. He will never be able to reach his full potential while he still has that weakness. Lucy behaves as a Kantian, then, when she cares more about Linus's duty to self-improvement than she does about his feelings. Improving yourself means more than simply doing the bare minimum.

When Linus talks about his recent ability to get through school without any mishaps, Lucy corrects him by saying, "You think being average is enough, don't you? Well it isn't! What shape would the world be in today if everyone settled for being average?" Lucy could easily placate Linus's need for encouragement, but as his older sister, she feels it's more important to play her role and do her duty to prepare him for the real world. In her eyes, this will serve society better because Linus will contribute in healthy ways to the overall economic stability and success of a responsible human citizen doing their part.

Phonies and Realies

One of quirkiest aspects of Kant's theory (one that many contemporary Kantians now reject), is that it is *never* permissible to tell a lie. Even if a killer comes to your door asking for the whereabouts of his intended victim, who, as it turns out, is hiding in your basement. You must tell him the truth. You may think that this sounds counterintuitive. Surely there are some things that we *ought* to lie about.

Remember that Kant thinks that it is immoral to make an exception of yourself. He also thinks that it's immoral to use people as mere means to your own ends. Lying violates both of these obligations. Kant believes that when you either give someone false information or withhold information from them, you are treating them as a means to your own ends. You aren't giving them the information that they need to make fully autonomous decisions.

When you're fully committed to the idea that you should *never* lie, or even withhold information, people might start to think that you are kind of rude. They might think you are blunt, or arrogant. Does this sound like anyone Charlie Brown knows?

Lucy is committed to telling the truth, come what may, or at least what she takes to be the truth (she is often mistaken about what the truth really is, and the patience that evidence collection calls for is not exactly her strong suit). She can't stomach people that don't have similar commitments.

> LUCY: Everywhere you go you seem to run into phonies! The people you think are sincere usually turn out not to be, and the people you think aren't sincere usually turn out to be sincere! The question is, how do you tell the phonies from the realies?

Lucy is a realie. Perhaps a little *too much* of a realie. Let's look back on some of Lucy's most "honest" utterances. She never hesitates to tell her friends and family exactly what she thinks about them.

She tells Charlie Brown:

> You're probably the most wishy-washy person I have ever known! You're really not much use to anyone Charlie Brown! You're weak, and dumb, and boring, and hopeless!

Yes, Lucy is brutally honest. Sometimes this works out. The honest things that she has to say to Schroeder are probably pretty good for his self-esteem. The straightforward, if painfully blunt, critiques that she gives to Snoopy on his novels might help him to become a better writer—perhaps the best beagle author of all time. But the cold and callous way in which she dishes out truths to her brother and to Charlie Brown are probably *not* good for them in the long run.

Aaugh!

Maybe Lucy isn't such a rude, bossy, blunt, know-it-all after all. Maybe she is just a Kantian, committed, unyieldingly, to truth. But wait . . . What about the football trick? Isn't tricking Charlie Brown mercilessly simply a rotten thing to do? Probably. But is there a way to understand her actions as Kantian in this case as well?

For Kant, the way to determine whether an action is morally right or morally wrong is to look at the intention of the person who performed it. So we can't look simply at how Charlie feels when the ball is pulled away from him, yet again. After all, it might not be Lucy's intention to cause Charlie Brown pain or to make him feel stupid or silly.

The best spin we could put on her actions is that, on each occasion, she is intending to do something other than deceive him. In the first set of strips in which the football gag appears, Lucy pulls her hand away, not to make a fool of Charlie Brown, but instead because she is worried that he will kick her hand. Shortly thereafter, she claims that she pulled the football away at the last minute to demonstrate Charlie Brown's unwavering faith in humanity. On yet another occasion, she claims, as his psychiatrist, that resolution of his psychological issues requires that he continue to attempt to kick the ball.

At the end of the day, though, it's tough to actually believe that Lucy's stated intentions are her *real* intentions. Sometimes she outright lies to Charlie Brown about whether she intends to pull the ball away at the last minute. On other occasions, she simply fails to give him the information he needs to make an informed choice about his situation. If he were acting on full and accurate information, he likely wouldn't attempt to kick the football at all.

But who knows? Hope springs eternal. In any event, despite attempts that Lucy might try to make to justify why her behavior is not simply mean spirited, in the final analysis, what matters is not what you say your intentions are. What matters is what your intentions *actually are.* Moreover, Lucy isn't behaving like a good Kantian if she doesn't tell the truth.

So is Lucy a Kantian or just a blunt, mean person? You've seen the argument for the former, and the strip certainly isn't short on arguments for the latter. We'll leave that for you to decide. Surely, if she's acting on Kantian impulses, she'd benefit from a philosophy class or two that might help her to be a better Kantian.

V

Is Kissing a Dog Really That Bad?

15
We're on Your Side, Charlie Brown

VERENA EHRNBERGER

Charlie Brown's relationship with his friends is somewhat complicated. Occasionally, the girls agree that good ol' Charlie Brown is a "good fellow." On the other hand, Chuck's universe is populated by children, and children behave immaturely—their behavior is often mean. Lucy won't let him kick the football (ever), and during their famous baseball match in *Charlie Brown's All-Stars* all of the kids agree that he's a "blockhead." Charlie Brown is the kid everybody picks on when things go wrong.

We wouldn't be surprised if Charlie Brown held all of this against his friends. But, interestingly enough, he doesn't. For example, in the *All-Stars* TV special, Charlie Brown doesn't want to hurt his friend's feelings and protects them from the truth that their potential sponsor wants Snoopy and the girls off the team. Why does he do that?

Charlie Brown is more mature than most of the other kids. But the oftentimes cruel behavior of his friends hurts him anyway. The girls make a sport out of not inviting him to their parties, Violet tells him that she never ever wants to see him again on a regular basis, and Lucy always tricks him when he attempts to kick the football.

Even when children aren't outright mean to him, they often do not have his best interests in mind. Schroeder's main focus is always on his piano, Linus is more skilled than

Charlie Brown in everything Charlie Brown shows him to do (folding a boat, building a house of cards, playing with a basketball), and Snoopy is oftentimes more concerned about his supper than he is about Charlie Brown and is even unable to remember his master's name, referring to him as "that round-headed kid." Good grief!

Still, Charlie Brown doesn't abandon his friends. And, although we are on Charlie Brown's side, we wouldn't advise him to abandon them either. Why does Charlie Brown keep putting up with this gang of oftentimes mean children? And why is it that we, as his fans, wouldn't want him to decide otherwise?

Friendship Means Loyalty

Charlie Brown's loyalty is one of the traits that makes him so lovable. Charlie Brown is a good guy, and this doesn't even change in the face of difficult and unfair situations. That's one of the reasons why we love seeing him go through these situations with his friends: he keeps his kind and loyal heart. No matter what. And this makes him exactly the kind of person we, as fans, feel comfortable being loyal to.

At the core of the concept of friendship lies the idea of loyalty. We tend to have a strong feeling of support and belonging for our friends. We support them because of their individual character, and this means that we don't have to agree with everything they think or do. Even if we don't share each of their opinions and can't relate to every way they chose to act, we are loyal to them anyways. We respect their values and principles, even if we don't share all of them.

Friendship is more than mere respect for people in general and more than respect for a particular person because of his or her merits; it is affection towards a particular person because of his or her peculiarity. Friendship acknowledges the uniqueness of the friend. We love our friends for who they are. And our friends, in return, are happy to be loved for their own sake. This affection brings us to feel a commitment towards our friends which expresses itself in our willingness to care about their needs, to act in their best interests and to take them seriously. And this is what loyalty is all about: we have a commitment towards a particular person, irrespective of abstract moral principles that may otherwise rule our lives. We're on their side, even if the moral principles we care about conflict with their views.

There's More than One Reason for Friendship

Friendship is all about balance. We want to give but we also want to receive something in return. The things that we give have to be balanced, but they don't have to consist in the very same thing. Charlie Brown gives his friends patience and kindness. But the others don't have to give the same kind of thing back.

Lucy gives Charlie Brown challenging checkers games and psychiatric advice. Snoopy gives him someone he can care for and someone who is always around (even if he hates Snoopy being around when eating candy). Linus is a good listener and an interesting conversational partner. Charlie Brown loves to have important discussions about life with Linus while standing up against the brick wall. And Schroeder plays classical music to Charlie Brown on his piano. So, it's important that both friends give something equivalent to keep the relationship balanced. But it doesn't have to be the very same thing.

Friendship is a relationship based on equality and reciprocity. As equals, friends should be able to show mutual respect towards the opinions of the other, and mutual affection and interest towards each other. In short, being friends means taking what our friends care about seriously. Schroeder knowns that Charlie Brown respects his love of Beethoven. And Charlie Brown would read the life of Beethoven to him when Schroeder was younger, because he cares about his friend's interest. Or take Charlie Brown and Linus: The two often support each other when one is feeling vulnerable. Especially when the Great Pumpkin doesn't show up on Halloween, Charlie Brown is there for his friend

Linus, who has been sitting in a pumpkin field the whole night. Although Charlie Brown does not believe in the Great Pumpkin himself, he supports Linus' beliefs and takes his quest for the Great Pumpkin seriously.

Friendship raises our sense for the feelings of others, enlarges our knowledge, enables us to make concessions we otherwise wouldn't make, and thereby empowers us to grow as human beings. That's why friendship is so important.

Ultimately, friendship is not about passing the time with someone or engaging in shared hobbies, but about a concept Marilyn Friedman calls "moral growth." All of us start out with the moral principles our family, especially our parents, taught us. In the course of our life we test these moral principles on individual situations. And oftentimes we realize that the moral principles of our family don't seem to fit the realities of our present world. So, there comes a point in every person's life where we're forced to re-evaluate our moral principles. And that's where our friends come in.

Our friends tell us about their experiences, their moral struggles and their solutions to a particular problem, and suddenly we have access to lots of experiences (beyond our own) we can learn from. The individual behavior of our friends in the difficult situations they had to face, opens up new perspectives for us. Like when Charlies Brown consults Lucy at her psychiatric booth about his deep feelings of depression, and she advises him to "snap out of it."

This advice might seem useless from a psychological point of view and is, of course, not an appropriate reaction to a clinical depression. But we have to assume that Charlie Brown is probably overacting and Lucy's reaction still shows him that there are other ways to deal with feelings of sorrow than to dwell on them. Through the eyes of our friends we learn to see the world from a different angle. Friends are therefore an invaluable source for the transformation of our abstract moral guidelines, and can contribute a lot to moral change.

In general, we trust our friends to be "reliable moral witnesses." This means we depend on people who are able to tell us about their experiences in an honest way to help us see things from their perspective, hence from a perspective that is different from our own. We take the moral principles they care about seriously, because we take our friends seriously. By learning from differing experiences and moral principles we are able to grow as human beings. This concept is known as "moral empiricism." We gain knowledge about the world by learning from our experiences, and, in the case of friendship, also by learning from the experiences of our friends.

This means that we have to know what our friends consider "good" or "bad" and that we should understand their perspective on moral values. When Lucy tells Charlie Brown to snap out of his depression during their psychiatry session, Charlie Brown has to trust that Lucy knows what she's talking about.

But how similar do our moral values have to be for us to experience moral growth through our friends? An old saying, "Birds of a feather flock together," points out that people with similar interests and needs tend to get on well with each other. But similar perspectives yield similar moral values, and therefore lead to less opportunity for moral growth. Friends who always agree with our perspective on life will never provoke the transformation of the abstract moral guidelines that we inherit from our families.

On the other hand, it's the similarity with our friends that leads us to trust them in the first place. A good friendship which sparks moral growth will therefore rest upon similarities as well as upon differences. But it is friendships that truly challenge the value system we believe in (like Charlie Brown's friendships) that will lead us to the most radical transformations of our moral guidelines and thereby lead to immense moral and personal growth.

Different Kinds of Friends

Friendship is a very broad term. And, since the advent of social media, the lines between who's a friend and who's a mere acquaintance have become even more blurry. As we have already seen, we are not friends with every one of our friends for the same reason. And we don't expect the same kind of friendship behavior from each and every one of them. So, it's a good thing that philosophers found categories to define friendship very early on.

According to Aristotle, friendship is a necessity and there's more than one kind of friendship. In fact, according to Aristotle, there are three: friendships based on utility, friendships based on pleasure, and friendships based on mutual good will. Friendships based on utility or pleasure are the kind of friendships that Aristotle calls the "imperfect.". They don't last long because we might change our interests and therefore seek pleasure from another friend, and utility changes according to the circumstances and so do the friendships based on it.

On the other hand, friendship based on mutual good will, Aristotle considers to be the "perfect" one. These friendships are based on the mutual desire of good for the friend's sake, and are cultivated between people who are good in themselves. Friendship of this kind is permanent, but needs time to develop. Apart from time, these friendships need intimacy because they can only develop when the friends have won their mutual trust. Of course, perfection is hard to achieve. As Aristotle says in his *Nicomachean Ethics*, "The wish for friendship develops rapidly, but friendship does not."

Aristotle points out that friendships based on pleasure are mainly found among the young, because their lives are regulated by their feelings, and their chief interest is their own pleasure. As the *Peanuts* are a society of children, this type of friendship seems to be fitting in their case. They play baseball together, work in Lucy's garden, throw parties, go trick-or-treating on Halloween, and perform in Christmas plays together. All these activities arise from their desire for pleasure, which therefore forms the foundation for their friendship.

According to Aristotle, friendship based on pleasure or utility is something only people of low character cultivate. But what kind of character are kids supposed to have? Is it even possible that children already have friendships based on good will?

Children are just starting to develop morals. They are still learning about right and wrong and are just in the process of forming a potentially good character. And they are influencing each other while they are growing up together. Therefore, those "imperfect" childhood friendships may very well provide a good foundation for "perfect" friendships, based on good will later in life. After all, kids growing up together with a good guy like Charlie Brown as their friend, will very likely adopt some of his good character traits. So, those "imperfect" childhood friendships might be a good starting point for future "perfect" ones based on "good will,"

Trust in Friendship

Trust, according to the philosopher Annette Baier, is accepted vulnerability to another's power to harm us. Trust is a space we give another person, and we leave it to them to decide how they are going to treat us. Of course, this other person might use this space to our disadvantage. And trust is an extremely vulnerable good which is "easily wounded and not at all easily healed." To keep a trust relationship healthy, it's important that all parties involved are capable of trust: which means that the truster is able to let go of control and let another person take care of something he or she cares about deeply, and that the trusted is able to treat the vulnerability of the other person with the appropriate diligence.

Lucy oftentimes calls Charlie Brown "gullible" (especially when she prevents him from kicking the football). She clearly uses this term pejoratively, but nothing's ever black-and-white. And while his gullibility clearly stands in his way from time to time, it also shows one other important thing: Charlie Brown is able to trust. And trust is such an important thing that the feeling of trust is considered a good by itself.

By trusting, Charlie Brown already enriches his life because he has a positive perspective on life—no matter how often Lucy takes away the football. If we, on the other hand, choose to see the world as an untrustworthy and hostile place, we ultimately only inflict damage on ourselves. This suspicious view of the world will hurt more in the long run, than landing on our backs from time to time, when somebody pulls away our football.

The belief in the good will of others allows us to live in a friendly atmosphere, which is, by far, a better outlook on life than living day by day in an atmosphere of suspicion and distrust. Charlie Brown keeps on trusting and doesn't let his frequent failures get in the way of becoming great. He is always confident that his baseball team still has a chance of winning, even if it almost never does. He only gets rocks when he goes trick-or-treating on Halloween but never loses hope that he will someday get candy.

Of course, everything has limits. Trust is not always a good thing that should be preserved in any case. It must be worthwhile for the parties involved. There are situations where trust is simply uncalled for. If we get disappointed again and again and get nothing at all in return from the people we're trusting with our vulnerability, then it might be time to call it a day. As far as friendship with Lucy is concerned, being friends with someone who pulls away the football when Charlie Brown is trying to kick it, but still plays with him and gives him valuable advice from time to time, doesn't seem like the worst choice. Charlie Brown knows he can't trust Lucy with the football. But he knows that he can trust her with lots of other things.

When it comes to the important stuff, Charlie Brown can always trust his friends in the end. They pick on him because of the baseball game in "Charlie Brown's All Stars," but they make him a manager uniform. They mock his tiny Christmas tree in "A Charlie Brown Christmas," but try hard to see Christmas from his perspective—they decorate the Christmas tree, showing him that this holiday is ultimately about love, not consumerism. In the end, Charlie Brown can always trust his friends to be there for him. And to appreciate his efforts.

The complicated friendships Charlie Brown has, seem to be worth preserving, because in the end he can always count on his friends to take his side.

Imperfect Friendship

We are not perfect. And we're not perfect friends. Oftentimes, in real life, this fact doesn't go unpunished. Friendships break off as easily as relationships do, especially in our society, where the idea of achieving more and being better than others, seems to apply even to our more important personal relationships. So, it is a comforting thought that people like Charlie Brown are out there—people who don't throw friendships away simply because their friends have been selfish and immature, people who are able to forgive and give second, third, and nth chances.

Charlie Brown always means well and cares deeply about his friends and family, and he's the first one to forgive if things are going wrong. He gives us the space to be imperfect, to laugh at his misadventures, while knowing he will never abandon us. We can rely on his kindness, and this fact gives us a feeling of stability—just like Linus's security blanket. Snoopy, too, is Charlie's Brown's friend, but not a lot can be expected out of him—he is after all, just a dog, even if he likes to demand to be more than that.

16
European Intellectuals Follow Charlie Brown!

MARIO BARILE AND PAOLO DINI

One of the keys to the success of *Peanuts* is its ability to be equally enjoyable to children and adults—and also intellectuals. Schulz's strips and the movies derived from them have been making us laugh for over half a century, but the laughter always leaves room for serious reflection.

In Schulz's work, the use of humorous devices such as repetition, absurdity, ambiguity and exaggeration is instrumental for conveying further meanings, beyond laughter and a sense of empathy. In 1965 the philosopher Umberto Eco introduced the first issue of the Italian magazine *linus*, describing Charlie Brown's comics as a "very important and serious thing" and acknowledging their cultural and literary value. Many readers have found important philosophical, psychological, and sociological insights in *Peanuts*.

That said, would you ever have expected to take leadership and management lessons from poor old Charlie Brown and his dysfunctional baseball team? Let's start with a look at the *Peanuts* gang as a microcosm.

Two Views of the *Peanuts* Microcosm

During his entire life, Charles Monroe Schulz drew nothing but children. In 1950, when the daily *Peanuts* strip first appeared, the choice to use children as the strip's main characters was not particularly original, nor were their adventures. In fact, Charlie Brown, Lucy, Linus and their friends are ordinary children living in an ordinary North American neighborhood and doing ordinary things, such as playing amongst themselves, going to school, or watching television. What makes Schulz's work unique, other than its global popularity, is his ability to give a mass medium like a comics strip artistic, philosophical, literary and sociological relevance.

In his 1964 book *Apocalittici e Integrati* (Apocalyptic and Integrated Intellectuals), Umberto Eco analyzes mass culture production as a result of the spread of mass media. According to Eco, the mass culture industry has replaced traditional bottom-up popular culture. Consumer music, books, and TV programs generally do not offer any stimulus for reflection. Rather, they reflect the dictates of the ruling power, giving the audience a temporary escape from everyday life while reinforcing current myths, norms, and values.

As in the past, when artists had to negotiate freedom of expression with censors, artistic expression still has constraints. However, some artists, thanks to their talent, succeed in conveying original, critical or liberating meanings, and Charles Schulz was one of them.

In the introduction to the first issue of *linus,* the first Italian magazine completely focused on comics, Umberto Eco interviewed two Italian writers, Elio Vittorini and Oreste Del Buono, trying to place *Peanuts* appropriately within American literature. Schulz was compared to J.D. Salinger; however, his work was described as more poetic. According to Vittorini, in *Peanuts* the world of children is a means to represent universal meanings, while in Salinger's work it is a mere escape from reality through literature.

From Eco's viewpoint, on a superficial and partial reading *Peanuts* portrays an idyllic children's world where Charlie Brown and his friends banter and make jokes in a light and funny way. A deeper, more reflective reading exposes Schulz's poetics emerging from the repetition of patterns and schemes. These, according to Eco, describe a microcosm that shows glimpses of the human condition: for example, he sees the *Peanuts* characters turning into little monsters as one of the negative effects of urban and industrial civilization on children.

At the heart of the vast majority of narratives is Charlie Brown, a sensitive child desperately searching for social acceptance and company but constantly failing, repulsed and bullied by the others. The tragic element in Charlie Brown's character is that he reflects the average person: a pure heart trying in vain to adapt to the formulas accepted by modern society, such as being a cherished entertainer or capturing girls' attention.

Charlie Brown's worst nightmare is Lucy, who probably best represents and assimilates contemporary values. She's self-confident, selfish, and perfidious. Together with her friends Patty and Violet, Lucy tries to escape from the contemporary human tragedy through alienation and heartlessness. Lucy's brother, Linus, is a science genius affected by emotional instability and able to feel at peace only when holding his blanket. Schroeder instead hides his neurosis behind an obsessive-compulsive passion for Beethoven and piano playing.

As a result of the passage of time and ancient civilizations, Pig Pen proudly gathers dust and dirt on his person. Even Snoopy shows maladjustment neuroses, through his dissatisfaction with being a dog and by constantly dreaming of being somebody else. In Eco's view, there are two reasons for Schulz's choice to portray a children's microcosm. On the one hand, it highlights the fact that industrial civilization has corrupted society from the roots; on the other hand, it leaves room for flashes of candor and optimism, that only children are still capable of.

Another interesting view of *Peanuts* as a microcosm comes from *Piccola Storia dei Peanuts,* the first monograph on *Peanuts*, published by Simona Bassano di Tufillo, an Italian cartoonist. Bassano di Tufillo describes Eco's analysis of the *Peanuts* microcosm as partial, as it was carried out while *Peanuts* was still in progress. According to Bassano di Tufillo,

Schulz's work highlights a wider philosophical conception of human beings in relation to nature than was observed by Eco.

To fully understand Bassano di Tufillo's perspective, we need to consider the concepts of *'distancing effect'* and individualism as they apply to *Peanuts*. Originally introduced by the literary critic Viktor Shklovsky, the distancing effect is an artistic method used to awaken a more authentic understanding of reality. This is to be contrasted with the automated perception of reality through routine.

In *Peanuts*, the use of children as main characters is considered by Bassano di Tufillo as a means to achieve a distancing effect, because children are new to the world and do not know its rules and habits. Together with the aim of strengthening the identification with the characters, this explains the total absence of adults in the strips. Another important element in Schulz's poetics is individualism and its relation to social solidarity.

On the one hand, difficulties in communication are among the most recurrent comedic aspects in *Peanuts*, and each character represents a monad, a single entity which is autonomous and unable to communicate with others. On the other hand, individualism does not lead to fights or isolation but to reciprocal acceptance and respect, shaping the concept of "sociable individualism." According to Bassano di Tufillo, this element of Schulz's poetics recalls the ideal of individualism, deeply rooted in American identity and culture, combined with a sense of community which has a strong American tradition too and is distant from selfish impulses. In fact, the *Peanuts* characters are always presented as a community, as a whole.

Schulz's sociable individualism includes not only human beings, but also animals and inanimate beings. In particular, Bassano di Tufillo considers *Peanuts* as an artistic representation of the vision conceived in the book *Mind and Nature* by the anthropologist Gregory Bateson. Bateson considers the human mind as part of the material world; therefore, its structure is no different from the universe's, including animals and inanimate beings. Leonardo da Vinci held a similar view with respect to the whole human body rather than just the mind: he saw the workings of the human body as a 'microcosm' of the 'universe' as it was perceived in the fifteenth century.

Similarly, in *Peanuts* animals, trees and schools think, and have their own personality. Nevertheless, they are not humanized as occurs in other cartoons such as Mickey Mouse. For Bassano di Tufillo, Schulz, while giving "voice and personality" to every part of creation, considers them as having the same dignity and importance as human beings. Therefore, Bassano di Tufillo attributes to Schulz an ecological message, even though in his work there are no explicit references to it.

Bateson's and Bassano di Tufillo's views can be related to the philosophical foundations of aboriginal spirituality. Although present in different forms in most human cultures, aboriginal spirituality is generally associated with Australia and Canada. These spiritual beliefs are based on conceiving the interconnectedness and interrelation among the elements of the Earth and the universe, both animate and inanimate. The foundations of aboriginal spirituality can be explained through the metaphor of a woven pattern representing the whole. This pattern has many colored threads, each of which represents a form of life. Each thread has the same importance as the others: a human is as important as a kangaroo or a rock. Therefore, the interconnectedness of all elements implies interdependence and inter-responsibility between them.

This philosophy has current practical consequences for the environment. For example, the traditional management of salmon runs in the wild rivers up to the coast of British Columbia is much more sustainable than Norwegian salmon farms along the same coast, which are market-driven and are destroying not only the local habitat but also the economy of the traditional and sustainable fisheries of the indigenous First Nations.

As we've seen, *Peanuts* is a meaningful microcosm from literary and philosophical perspectives. In addition, the

Peanuts gang is often engaged in team activities, the most popular of which is playing baseball: could we then consider it from an organizational perspective? In order to answer this question, we need to say a few things about the philosophy of management and some of the ideas at its foundation.

Peanuts and Philosophy of Management

One of the main concerns of the philosophy of management is to justify an organization's right to exist in the larger social system. In other words, how does an organization contribute to the community it is embedded in and to the common good? This is the issue of corporate legitimacy, which is at the core of the philosophy of management.

The philosophy of management also focuses on understanding what organizations are, the role of human beings in organizations, and the knowledge that is relevant to the study of organizations. In this regard, the philosophy of management blends theoretical knowledge with empirical observation and integrates different social sciences, such as sociology, economics, management and leadership.

Another important discussion concerns the complex relation between ethics and economics. Some economists, such as Adam Smith, argue that economic rationality, which implies self-interest and seeking profit maximization in markets, is a part of ethics. Thus, market actors, while seeking their own interest, will contribute to the common good. Therefore, fair competition and economic institutions could be adequate and sufficient to contribute to a better society.

Other approaches such as that of the sociologist Walter Powell state that even though economic rationality can inspire ethical values it is completely separate from ethics. From this perspective, in addition to economic rationality it is the personal values of individuals that have an impact on organizational behavior and contribute to shape business ethics, including moral values. The philosophy of management also focuses on the relation between art, creativity and management, because they are considered sources of innovation.

As we have seen with Bassano di Tufillo, the relation between the self and the other is a major topic in the *Peanuts* microcosm. In addition to relational, also organizational aspects emerge in Schulz's work. But can the *Peanuts* "community" be considered an organization?

The Online Business Dictionary defines an organization as "a social unit of people that is structured and managed to meet a need or to pursue collective goals". Thus, *Peanuts* can be defined as an organization, as Charlie Brown and his friends are often engaged in collective activities toward a common goal, most of which are baseball games.

The *Peanuts* baseball team has fairly well-defined roles under the management of Charlie Brown. In spite of that and of Charlie Brown's persistent efforts and optimism at the start of each season, the team achieves very poor results. Over fifty years of daily strips and several cartoon specials, Charlie Brown's team was able to win only about ten matches, most of which when its manager was not playing (very funny for us, but terribly disheartening for him). That is just one of the reasons why our favorite child is often blamed and bullied by his friends.

Even though the *Peanuts* gang is a group of peers and there are no real main characters, during their collective activities the issue of leadership is particularly evident and has a strong impact on the team.

Lucy versus Charlie Brown

In addition to baseball matches, the *Peanuts* gang is often engaged in organizing school recitals, especially during the Christmas holiday season. Charlie Brown and Lucy are the most recurrent leading personalities, and show opposite management styles. Lucy's leadership emerges, for example, in the 1985 cartoon "Sally's Sweet Babboo," where Charlie Brown writes an essay on his last Christmas. The essay is mainly about the Christmas play organized by Lucy. Lucy has a fixed and well-defined plan with roles and responsibilities for everyone (she being the star, of course). Many of the roles assigned are not tailored to her friends' personalities and skills. However, to Charlie Brown's and Linus's complaints, she responds: "Learn!" As a result, everyone feels under pressure and the play is a disaster, with everyone blaming . . . Charlie Brown. On the other hand, the 'round-headed kid' shows strong listening and mediation skills, even though his friends tend to ignore his suggestions. Charlie Brown is much more oriented towards pondering about the meaning and sense of his and his team's actions. He's generally committed, fairly assertive, and well prepared, but team harmony and unity are his main concerns.

These two leadership styles mirroring the respective personalities of Lucy and Charlie Brown can be related to the two modes of relating to people and things identified by Martin Heidegger in his work *Discourse on Thinking*.

Lucy's approach to the world can be defined as *calculative*. *Calculative thinking* is a form of thinking which emerged in the technological age, and refers to the human capacity to control, compute, and exploit things and people. This approach, focused on planning, research, and scientific organization, is considered instrumental to attaining power and profit. Rather than focusing on controlling and computing with the aim of maximizing self-interest, *reflective thinking* searches for the meaning and the directions of human actions in the world.

To understand this approach, it needs to be related to Heidegger's major work, *Being and Time*, which undertakes to understand how human beings interact with the world and what this means in relation to the finiteness of life. In Heidegger's view, living authentically means accepting and appropriating our individual and collective responsibilities towards ourselves and the world.

This search for sense is conditioned by our limited existence. Therefore, even though *calculative thinking* may be useful to achieve our everyday life objectives, we should use *reflective thinking* to discover the authentic meaning of our individual and collective involvement in the world, in order to find sense and direction. Rather than planning and controlling things and relations in order to achieve outcomes, we should be open to the "mystery" of our being-in-the-world, which is not always obvious or apparent to us.

Calculative and *reflective thinking* can also be applied to organizations. The former mirrors an approach strongly oriented towards efficiency, power and economic strength, which implies rigid organizational structures, roles and responsibilities. As the main goals are profits and outcomes, there is no room for change, creativity and innovation. Actually, this model seems to describe most organizations, which can be identified as 'inauthentic' in Heidegger's view.

By contrast, the *reflective organization* is focused on fostering and encouraging its members to search for their own possibilities by empowering and engaging them actively in setting goals, finding appropriate means, and even contributing to implement or revise corporate ends. Similarly, an 'authentic' organization does not regard its members as a means to efficiency, effectiveness and productivity, but cares for them and their diversity as they are ends in themselves. As a consequence, according to a Heideggerian perspective, profits are important but less important than personal and social values.

Heidegger's approach was applied to management and leadership only recently, as organizational behavior has always been paired with conformity; furthermore, traditional management theories define the leader as a person who is in control, rather than encouraging their fellow workers' search for their own authenticity. If Heidegger's view can be meaningfully applied to leadership and management, we believe that Charlie Brown and his baseball team represent it well. A clear example is shown in the TV special *Charlie Brown's All-Stars*.

Despite countless defeats, Charlie Brown receives a sponsor proposal which would guarantee a placement in an organized league and a new uniform (it would be an outstanding result for an amateur team). That news gives some hope to the team, which was about to abandon its manager. However, Charlie Brown decides to refuse the proposal after being asked to leave girls and Snoopy out of the team in order to join the league, as girls or dogs are not allowed. When he communicates the decision to his friends, not telling the reasons why, he causes girls' anger and complaints. Once Linus tells them the whole story, they present a uniform with the words "Our Manager" on the front to Charlie Brown, in order to make up for having been hard on him.

Peanuts has no happy ending, and Charlie Brown's team will never succeed. However, Charlie Brown teaches us that, even though results are important, human dignity, creativity and diversity are much more so.

Chuck, a Modern Leader

Even though he's not a protagonist, as Schulz wrote in 1975, Charlie Brown is "the focal point of almost every story." He is "the one who suffers, because he is the caricature of the average person." However, repetition and irony in *Peanuts* strips make him into a very complex character. On the one hand, he is a lovable loser: insecure, constantly failing, blamed and bullied by everyone. A genuine person in a cruel world, a kind of victim predestined. On the other hand, he is the only one who is able to keep his friends together.

That's particularly true of the baseball team. He's the boss not because of strong skills, charisma, or authoritarian attitude, but because of his exceptional ability to shape and safeguard a climate of tolerance, mutual respect, and freedom for everyone to seek his or her own authentic form of expression. As we have seen, it's a well-defined leadership style which can be compared to a Heideggerian approach to management.

The fact that Charlie Brown is and will always be a loser is a leitmotif which will make us laugh and love him forever. However, paradoxically, that leaves us another important and inspirational message: Never give up. Dealing with failure is a key to success.

17
Linus's Blanket

PETER COSTELLO

When *Peanuts* was in its heyday in the 1970s, when I myself was the age of its main characters, I remember feeling surprised, regularly surprised, on Sunday mornings to hear sermons at church that began with what happened to Charlie Brown, Lucy, and Linus.

Why would ministers or priests begin their no doubt profound comments on life and God by quoting a comic strip about children? Surely, I thought, Sunday services should be about something more intellectual, something more substantive. As a child myself, I needed to sit still. I shouldn't be able to understand God or life through *Peanuts,* through a comic strip I, a child, enjoyed reading.

As an adult, though, I see those attempts of the minister to include children in the sermon, both as subject and as audience, to be quite revelatory. Now I see what the minister may also have seen—namely, that Schulz's children, and indeed any children, are quite possibly the most astute posers of substantive questions. Children can sometimes make the best philosophers and prophets.

How do peanuts become philosophers or prophets, though? How do they pose the substantive question that resonates with the minister as well as the child? One thing to me seems certain: these children Schulz created speak out of *difficult* positions and situations. They are not simply happy and carefree. On the contrary, they have very complex emotional and personal lives. And they are forced to act and speak within situations (such as attending public school or playing little league baseball) that they did not exactly choose.

Indeed I believe it is *because of this fact,* it is because children speak out of their enforced, difficult positions, that they sometimes gain the possibility of becoming philosophers and therefore can demand our attention. Children live with our set-up of their lives as a stranger inhabiting a foreign land. And it is precisely the stranger who is sometimes in the best position to offer a comment on the land he or she has come to dwell in.

Because they did not set up the situations in which they dwell, then, children can come to challenge or transcend them. They can come to see our imposed situations as mere attempts by us adults to manage, sometimes to micromanage, the person who is really powerful—namely, the child who has to submit to this situation, this system, and be contained, for example in a church pew.

It is because of the possibility children have to *live with* their situations and even to resist or transcend the limitations that we adults impose upon them that children are capable of becoming profound philosophers.

A case in point is Linus, the little peanut who speaks most directly (and perhaps most often) about things we might see as philosophical—such as scripture passages or existential truths. Linus, the voice of wisdom, is in a tragicomic difficulty. For he, though in grade school, still carries a blanket. And thus we see that the figure of Linus, the prophet of *Peanuts,* is one that is profoundly moral, profoundly loyal, and profoundly stuck. His resistance to and transcendence of imposed, difficult situations (such as being the younger brother of Lucy) occurs by means of his own limited resource—his blanket.

The adults in *Peanuts*'s lives would have it that these children are quickly developing themselves into other adults. Adults would have it be the case that the children themselves accept that they already on the way to being an adult.

The adults, in short, would rather Linus give up the blanket and pull himself up by his own bootstraps.

To the adults that set up his world, and the pace for his development, it is unacceptable that Linus live his own way into the world at his own pace. It is meaningless that Linus invents metaphysical figures such as the Great Pumpkin. But Linus does not give in. He carries his blanket as the talisman of his own resistance and of his insights. He is philosophical because he sees by means of what is given to him toward the truth—namely, that what is set up answers to more than those who set it up in the first place.

And thus the retention of his blanket does not cancel out Linus's philosophical capacity. Rather, it's precisely Linus's insistence on the blanket, and his inability to live without it, that somehow allows him to become a philosophical speaker. It's his being "stuck" with the blanket that allows him to see more clearly into the structures that try to shape him from without. Finally, it's the life with the blanket that allows Linus to see into the difficult lives and perspectives of other children, perhaps especially into the story of Charlie Brown's unrequited love for the Little Red-Haired Girl.

The Psychology of Linus's Blanket

Psychologist Donald W. Winnicott is well-known for his description of early childhood—especially infancy—in terms of transitional objects. The most familiar transitional object is the blanket. The blanket is not itself transitional. Rather, the infant is. But the infant *uses* the blanket as he makes her transitions, as he moves toward his own perspective on the world as part of a network of other perspectives.

The blanket sets up a home for the infant to retreat to, psychically. The blanket is where he, the infant, can retreat and suck his thumb or caress a corner and thereby begin to rest from the exhaustion of being watched and being spoken to. The blanket is what allows the baby to move back and forth—to retreat from and return to a life with others and a self that is being stabilized within a family.

Linus's blanket, then, is for Winnicott "an intermediate area of experiencing, to which inner reality and external life both contribute. It is an area not to be challenged, because no claim is made on its behalf except that it shall exist as a resting-place for the individual engaged in the perpetual human task of keeping inner and outer reality separate yet interrelated" (*Playing and Reality*, p. 3). This is the "intermediate area" that Linus's blanket enables or represents.

All of us, perhaps especially children, have difficulty navigating the at-times-competing claims of our own internal way of living in a situation that we share with others. For we cannot just live our lives the way we want. The others' "external" views on our shared situation insist on entering into what is happening, even into our self-description. And any equilibrium we may have previously achieved with respect to our internal and external life seems regularly to be threatened with annihilation.

The blanket or babbling or bit of cloth that a baby "possesses" is what Winnicott focuses on as the child's "defence against anxiety, especially anxiety of a depressive type" (p. 5). Those with children or with experience of children notice that the baby is trying to have some "down time" by means of the blanket. We intuitively understand that it is tough for the infant to reckon with a complex world all by herself, with her limited resources. So we almost automatically allow the baby to have a corner of a world that is hers alone, that is not challenged, where she can be neither within nor without.

We allow the baby this space because she cannot yet talk or argue. She cannot yet make a claim on the blanket's behalf. And she should not have to do so, even if she could. By the *way* she holds on to it, we almost immediately see that she is not claiming that we *recognize* the blanket. Rather, she is, by this particular way of removing herself from the situation, implicitly claiming that we ought *not* to consider either her or the blanket, just as she is not considering it but rather rubbing or sucking on it in a way that suggests "zoning out."

In *Peanuts*, like the situation of the infant, I believe it is not really his blanket that is so important to the story or even to Linus but rather the *way* Linus relates to it, *where* he relates to it, and *who* he can be while holding it. Winnicott puts this point in terms of the self as the thing that is transitional: "It is not the object, of course, that is transitional. The object represents the infant's transition from a state of being merged with the mother to a state of being in relation to the mother as something outside and separate" (pp. 19–20). The blanket is the visibile token of Linus' transitional ability. The blanket is the way Linus can move between the children in *Peanuts*. It is Linus's way of expressing, without expressing, how he can move between them, the adults, and himself.

But Linus is no infant. And no other child his own age in *Peanuts* has anything like a blanket, a transitional object. At best, Pigpen hides in his cloud of dust. But that is not something that either helps or hinders Pigpen's movement in the group. What then are we to make of Linus and his transitional object that seems empowering long after it should have been the case that Linus gave it up?

According to Winnicott, there is a natural point at which the infant lets go of the transitional object. This time of letting-go is not marked by any special memory or ritual: "it is not forgotten and it is not mourned. It loses meaning, and this is because the transitional phenomena have become diffused, have become spread out over the whole intermediate territory, between inner psychic reality and the external world as perceived by two persons in common, that is to say over the whole cultural field" (2005, 7). The blanket loses meaning as a cloud of dust disperses into the air. It is no longer visible as itself but it has spread its influence and power throughout the area in which one stands.

Linus, however, appears stuck. He cannot allow the blanket to stop having a meaning. He uses it to protect himself, to calm himself, to occupy a space set apart and thus to become profound. The blanket is thereby, as the object of a stuck child, also the site of challenge—Snoopy, for example, lunges at it and yanks it around and around; even Lucy attempts to humiliate and demoralize Linus for the ongoing attachment.

Linus thus does more with the blanket than the infant does. Linus *resists and transcends* by means of the blanket. And thus he calls attention to what should never be called attention to—i.e., that something is not working in the adult systems that have been set up for the children in *Peanuts*. Something is ineffective in the way holidays are set up, the way education is set up, the way families are set up. Each mother is absent. Have we ever seen her? Each father is absent. Have we ever seen him? We cannot even hear the adults except as a kind of mwah-mwah sound.

How is Linus supposed to give up the blanket when something has gone terribly wrong in his world? On which adult can he depend for help?

Even Winnicott seems to acknowledge Linus's difficulty. For Winnicott does say that it is clear that no one, not even a healthy adult, is "free from the strain of relating inner and outer reality, and that relief from this strain is provided by an intermediate area of experience . . . which is not challenged (arts, religion, etc.)" (*Playing and Reality*, p. 13).

As largely healthy adults, then, we have moved from a transitional object, from our own role as blanket-holders, to a whole realm of transitional phenomena. We have created sermons and written books in philosophy. Our relation with the blanket has diffused into our relation with art or religion or philosophy. And we can begin, when we create art or enter into religion or philosophy, to address in a more lasting and *now meaningful way* the relationship between our inner and outer experience.

But Linus is not an adult. He's a child. And Linus does not have others with whom he can yet develop and diffuse the transitional object into a world of art and religion. Sally, for example, joins him in the pumpkin patch only because she loves him—not because she sees what Linus sees.

Nevertheless, even though Linus does not successfully inaugurate a new holiday or a new mode of worship for others, he is the closest one of all the peanuts to true philosophy. For, in the world of *Peanuts*, it is the character of Linus who offers his transitional object, his relation with his blanket, and his transitional realms of religion, art and philosophy in order to facilitate the group of children in *Peanuts* becoming a more self-sufficient, supportive, and responsive community of friends. It is precisely the most profoundly stuck among them who proves to be the most mature.

Love and Transition

The movie *You're in Love, Charlie Brown* reveals how Linus moves between the children in order to allow them to relate to each other, to themselves, and to something that surpasses them all.

The movie *You're in Love, Charlie Brown* begins with Charlie Brown being disappointed with Snoopy for not serving him breakfast and with his mother, presumably, for packing peanut butter sandwiches again in his lunch bag. Immediately after this expression of Charlie Brown's dissatisfaction with a lack of friends and of good food, we see him calling attention to Linus's blanket. He wonders whether Linus is worried about what kids at school will say. Linus asks Charlie Brown if he has a nickel and then proceeds to zap it with the blanket when Charlie Brown throws it into the air. Linus then says that the other children usually don't say very much about Linus's blanket. They do not challenge it.

It may seem surprising that the beginning of this movie about Charlie Brown's love is about his initial dissatisfaction and then with his preoccupation with Linus's relation to his own blanket. However, if we take to heart Winnicott's discussion of transitional objects, we see at least one reason why this beginning makes sense: Linus *does have* a transitional object with which he navigates the world and his place in it. Charlie Brown, however, does not.

And it is precisely his lack of a sufficient transitional object that generates all the tension and depression for much of the movie—and generates our emotional identification with Charlie Brown. Linus is not wholly dissatisfied and thus is not looking to be entrapped in a total, external, unrequited love that would display his internal state for all to see. Charlie Brown, on the other hand, is *completely* dissatisfied and, therefore, stuck pursuing an external confirmation of his internal dissatisfaction. Charlie Brown *wants* to be trapped so that he and others can see what his own internal emotional life is like.

As they walk, Charlie Brown discusses what he would like—"an enjoyable pleasant lunch." But of course he cannot have this. So total is his dissatisfaction that Charlie Brown cannot enjoy even the basic act of eating. Presumably this is because he feels no comfort, no recognition, no certainty that anyone likes him.

In fact, immediately after this second expression of dissatisfaction, Charlie Brown sees the Little Red-Haired Girl passing on a bus, and he points her out to Linus. Why can't he have lunch with her?

This fascination with the beloved, who is never named, continues within the school. Charlie Brown starts to write her a letter but mistakenly reads it as one of the pages of his school report. What was meant to be private or internal becomes public and external, and the effort to bring his internal desire to fruition explodes in laughter. The external and the internal merge horribly. There is no escape, no transitional area. He just is his situation. There is no transcending it.

Linus, however, with his trusty blanket at his side, has no problem in finding others to love him. In fact, Sally insists on loving him so much that Linus even puts the blanket over his head at the bottom of the slide to prevent her from getting too close. We're almost tempted to think that it's *because* he has a blanket that Linus is able to secure love from others.

The Nameless Love Object

When Charlie Brown seems unable to introduce himself to the Little Red-Haired Girl, he wants Linus to act as intermediary. He wants Linus to act "real sly" and figure out if she likes Charlie Brown. But Linus appears incapable of deception. He simply tells the girl that Charlie Brown is madly in love with her.

Linus's Blanket

What Charlie Brown is incapable of doing, stating his feelings and meeting another person on his own two feet, on his own terms, Linus has no problem doing. Linus inhabits the same world as Charlie Brown and yet is able to navigate it and perceive it differently.

This difference in perception is most noticeable when Charlie Brown and Linus share the newly-painted bench at lunchtime. Charlie Brown is unable to recognize that Linus is his friend and sharing the bench with him. Instead, Charlie Brown talks about how the Little Red-Haired Girl can't see him because he's "nothing." Linus has not seen Charlie Brown as nothing, but then Linus sees the playground as a horizon of possibilities (games and eating) and not as a prison in which to bemoan his horrible plight.

The nothingness that Charlie Brown takes himself to be noticeably affects his ability to eat. The peanut butter sandwich is something that he "ties into a knot," as Linus says. Charlie Brown of course blames "unrequited love" and we thus see his inability to move away from his anxiety even while alone. Again, there is no transitional object, no transitional space. Charlie Brown's depression, or whatever it is he lives with and as, appears to be diffused everywhere. His lack of a transitional object means that what is diffused is nothingness, is dissatisfaction, instead of empowerment.

When it seems to Charlie Brown that the Little Red-Haired Girl is approaching his bench, Charlie Brown does something similar to Linus's move with the blanket at the bottom of the slide. Charlie Brown puts his lunch bag over his head. However, the bag is not a transitional object as Linus' blanket is. The bag has no power to mediate the world and his own anxiety.

With the bag on his head, Charlie Brown bumps into Lucy who says he is "ridiculous." This contrasts with Linus's move with his object, the blanket, which, while over his head, mysteriously guides Linus through a number of children swinging.

At the end of the last day of school, we see Charlie Brown rushing to the bus for his last chance to meet the Little Red-Haired Girl. He misses her, and we see Linus as the last one of the crowd to get on the bus. Mysteriously, as Charlie Brown bemoans his fate, we see a letter in Charlie Brown's hand. It is from the Little Red-Haired Girl, and we know this since the signature is "the Little Red-Haired Girl."

This transitional object, the letter, does not name her. As she was in the beginning of the movie, she remains on the border between general and particular. And the letter only says that she likes him.

This permits the letter to serve as a transitional object. And Charlie Brown clutches this letter as if it were a blanket on the way home. It is sure to see him through the summer until school starts, he implies, and we wonder who could have known to have given Charlie Brown this talisman that would allow him to have some distance between his external and internal experiences. Perhaps a certain person who has just such a thing. Perhaps Linus.

Prophet of the Great Pumpkin

If Linus retains his blanket as a kind of pathological hold on transitional space and relationality, he also serves as a kind of philosopher or prophet. For it is Linus who helps the Charlie Brown Christmas tree by wrapping the blanket around the base. And it is Linus, who, with his blanket, asks for the spotlight on the school stage. Lifting his blanket in the air to emphasize his words, it is Linus who recounts the gospel nativity story.

Linus's diffusion of the transitional into religion is also not limited to his prophetic utterances from scripture or his care for the tree. He also creatively invents the Great Pumpkin.

The space between Halloween and Christmas is a kind of rather anxious waiting for many children. In eager anticipation, Linus has pre-maturely called up a vision of Santa Claus with some version of a more ancient religion, a religion of the Earth and of its produce, in his expectant creation of and his waiting for the Great Pumpkin.

So compelling is Linus's account of the Great Pumpkin that Sally goes to wait with him in the pumpkin patch. But it is his claims in the face of others' disbelief that doom Linus. He does not allow others to find their "overlapping" creative possibilities in his religiousness. He tries to win them back from "tricks or treats" into something that they do not, on their own, recognize as having equal value. Rather, he tries to claim them by virtue of their self-interest or guilt, and thus failure results.

Linus's creation of the Great Pumpkin, however, shows what his main feature is. He is loyal. He is faithful. He is loyal to scripture, to his own creativity, and to his "sincerity...as far as the eye can see."

This loyalty comes out as his very singular enactment of what it means to live a meaningful life. And it does not fail to impress upon his circle of friends something that every other one of them lacks in some important way.

Linus, with his blanket, is so often the act of transition itself. He moves between friends, defending one here, cheering one up there. He moves by attempting to understand, by attempting to exhort. He takes a role that no other child can have by virtue of his shaping his life according to the more adult themes and views that are announced in Scripture and in the person of the teacher or the parent or the minister.

Linus's self is what Winnicott might perhaps call the "good enough self." Yes, he carries the blanket too long. The blanket does not lose meaning when it should have done so. And yet the meaning of this transitional object spreads from the blanket throughout Linus' experience of the world.

Where Linus must grow is toward the enactment of loyalty and fidelity to his own limited life as a human being. His blanket is not a replacement for his mother or the adult figures in his life. His blanket cannot navigate all the problems that arise when we enter a shared world. We need others to help us do that—others who have greater facility and experience. We need adults.

If Linus were to have an ongoing support system of adults, his relationship with the blanket would lose meaning. If Linus were not the only one seeing metaphysical implications to holidays, he would not need the blanket to "have his back."

We know, as adults, that Linus's sincerity and loyalty do not arise as magical epiphenomena of his relationship to this object, this blanket. Rather, the blanket is simply the place-holder for the movement of loyalty and fidelity that Linus is already making. So his anxiety at losing the blanket (as in *A Boy Named Charlie Brown*) definitely deserves his attention and ours.

We adults who view *Peanuts* need to share with our own children and with each other the lesson that Linus offers. It is too much for one person to be the conscience of the community. It is too much for one person only to be loyal and moral. Rather, such a project must be shared.

It all comes down to this, as perhaps Snoopy's repeated attacks on the blanket bring to light: no matter how well Linus navigates the world, he cannot fully become an adult until the blanket fully evaporates or disperses into the air, into the community, around him. Certainly, Snoopy and the others remind Linus that the blanket itself, as a way of moving toward transitional space, will never cease also to be a site of possible vulnerability. Once this vulnerability is something Linus can acknowledge, once we adults learn how to approach him and support him in his vulnerability, his transition to a more adult stage will accomplish itself.

How Grown-Ups Learn from Peanuts

By looking at *You're in Love, Charlie Brown* and focusing on Linus and his blanket we can highlight what is meaningful in *Peanuts* and in Charles Schulz's presentation of childhood. The characters of Charlie Brown, Linus, Lucy, Snoopy and the others are reaching beyond their limited means, but out of their own resources, into adult shapes of perception and experience. Living within the situations adults have set up for them, their resistance and transcendence embody something important about what it means to exist as a human being.

We too, we adults, learn from them. We learn from children. For we too are never simply done adjusting to the world or to each other. We too, even as adults, are transitional beings. We are on the way. We are becoming. We have our depressions, our aggressiveness, our transitional spaces, and our attempts at forming a circle of friends.

We too have difficulty eating and sleeping, loving and being loved. We too worry about whether someone like Schroeder or the Little Red-Haired Girl really like us. We too would like a pleasant lunch, a reliable religion, a meaningful experience of holidays and of education and of home.

We may no longer need a blanket. But we do need continuously to move toward more adult shapes of living by using what we have here and now, with those sitting on the bench alongside us.

18
No End to Philosophy

RACHEL ROBISON-GREENE

In this book, we've heard a lot about Lucy's psychiatry booth, Charlie's little league team, and Linus' belief in the Great Pumpkin. We've read about the ways that friendship and existential angst are portrayed in the *Peanuts* universe. There are some characters, however, that we haven't heard much about.

The *Peanuts* universe is delightfully quirky, and the strip went on for many years. Many of these quirky happenings present interesting philosophical questions and ideas. Let's look back and enjoy some of those moments in the form of a few short philosophical *Peanuts* vignettes.

Sally Finds Meaning in the Universe

Absurdity is a concept that is popular in the work of existentialist thinkers. Different philosophers have different definitions of the concept. Famously, Albert Camus defined absurdity as, roughly, a confrontation between the desires of individual human beings and an indifferent universe.

Humans, almost universally, desire things that the universe doesn't supply. We want to be significant, and yet the universe is so large that, proportionally, we are no more significant than specks of dust. The universe has lasted so long, and will continue to last for so much longer, that our individual dealings in it are blips on the radar—of no real importance.

We long for immortality, and yet we all must eventually die. We long for justice. We want to see good people rewarded and we want to see the guilty punished. What's more, when we take it upon ourselves to dedicate our lives to becoming good people, we want to see that dedication validated. But the universe simply does not care. It simply isn't the kind of thing that can care. The absurdity of the human condition is that we are condemned to be caring beings in an uncaring universe.

That's all very depressing. But it has the potential to set up a good gag in a comic strip. What would it be like if the universe *could* care about the deepest longings of our hearts? If not the universe as a whole, what if just a *segment* of the universe could muster up some interest in the petty problems of human beings? Enter the most bizarre character in the *Peanuts* universe—The School Building.

The School Building is, of course, the place where most of the *Peanuts* characters attend school (with the exception of Peppermint Patty, Franklin, and Marcie, who go to a school across town). In addition to this traditional role, The School Building also takes a particular shine to Sally and looks over her. Sally begins talking to the building in a strip from July 1971. At that point, it seems indifferent to her, just like the rest of the universe. Perhaps it's because she is shouting at it that it has no power over her during summer vacation.

Later, in 1974, she spends several strips berating the school. She finally softens and reports that she likes the school's bricks. It replies with a thought bubble containing a heart.

The previously indifferent School Building has finally taken an interest in the world around it—at least when it comes to Sally Brown. Later, when Sally introduces Linus to the building as "her boyfriend," the school thinks, "You better treat her well . . . I'm the jealous type. The building even goes so far as to drop bricks on the heads of people that get on Sally's bad side.

Isn't this what we are all after? For the seemingly indifferent universe to take an interest in our lives and our insignificant problems? I don't know about you, but I could stand to see a brick or two drop once in a while . . .

Reclaiming Identity—3, 4, and 5

In 1963, Schulz introduced some rather unusual characters into the *Peanuts* universe in the form of 3, 4, and 5. We learn in a strip from 1963, that the surname of these characters is 95472. 5 insists that to pronounce the surname correctly, you must put the emphasis on the "4." 3 and 4 appear to be identical twin sisters, and 5 is their older brother.

Why the unusual surname? 5 explains in a strip from September 30th 1963. He claims that his father is concerned that the prevalence of numbers in society is depriving people of their identities. As a form of protest, he changed the names of his family members to numbers. Their last name is actually a zip code—specifically the zip code for Sebastopol, California, where Schulz was living at the time.

What are we to make of 5's father's claim? What *is* identity, and why might someone think that the prevalence of numbers in society might undermine it? We all seem to have some sort of common-sense working notion of what identity is. We tend to think that we retain our identities over time. Despite the fact that we go through substantial change throughout the course of our lives, we're still the same people that we were at earlier points.

Our common-sense ideas about identity might not be entirely justified. Consider the thought experiment frequently referred to by philosophers as "The Ship of Theseus." Imagine that there is a ship that is about to begin a voyage. It's Theseus's ship and we have no record of its name—maybe the ancient Greeks didn't name their ships—so we just call it "The Ship of Theseus."

The ship departs from the harbor in perfect working order. The voyage is long, and as the ship travels, its construction begins to falter and bits of it fall to the bottom of the ocean. By the time the ship is taken out of commission after it's lengthy stint at sea, all its parts, one by one, have fallen to the bottom of the sea and have been replaced with new parts. Now imagine that all of the old parts are collected from the bottom of the sea. A ship is constructed from the collected parts. We now have two ships, one of which is the ship that ended the voyage, and the other is a ship constructed from all of the original parts that The Ship of Theseus had when it departed from the harbor.

The question is, which ship is The Ship of Theseus? Is it the ship constructed from the original parts? Is it the ship that finished the voyage? Is it both? Is it neither? Notice that this is a question that is fundamentally about identity and persistence through time. Did the ship somehow retain its identity as each of its parts was changed? How is this possible?

It's s tricky question, and it doesn't just apply to ships. We, ourselves, have changed dramatically since the time of our births. Our bodies have changed, our cells have died and have been regenerated. Our beliefs, attitudes, and sentiments have (hopefully) changed dramatically since we were small children. What makes us who we are, and are we correct in claiming that we remain the same people through time? If so, how is this possible?

There are several different positions. Some have argued that the thing that makes us who we are—the thing that allows our identities to persist through time—is our immortal souls. Because individuals have the same soul from one moment to the next, it follows that the person is the same person from one moment to the next.

I won't spend time here discussing the arguments for and against the existence of a soul. Instead, let's look at another problem posed by this account of identity. When Linus sees Charlie Brown from across the schoolyard, he is able, effectively and consistently, to accurately identify him. How is it, if the same-soul account of identity is true, that Linus is so good at this? It can't be that Linus is accurately identifying Charlie Brown's soul on each occasion. The immaterial soul is not something that can be observed with the naked eye (or by any of the physical senses, really). The same-soul, same-person account of personal identity can't account for Linus's ability to consistently accurately identify Charlie Brown and his other friends.

A second account of personal identity can adequately explain how we can consistently and accurately recognize one another. We'll call it the same body, same person position. The view is exactly what it sounds like. If a person has the same body through time, they are the same person. The reason that Linus can identify Charlie Brown from across the schoolyard is that he recognizes Charlie's body.

There are also a number of problems with this position. First of all, people's bodies change dramatically all the time, for a variety of reasons. What does "same body" mean? It's not clear that any of us actually *have* the same body that we had when we were babies. Furthermore, when we introduce sci-fi type thought experiments into the discussion, it becomes obvious that the same body criterion might not do the job. Imagine that an evil scientist kidnaps two people, let's call them Jane and Sarah, and switches their brains? When Jane's body contains Sarah's brain, do we want to say that Sarah now occupies the body? If so, the same body criteria doesn't seem to work either.

Another common account of identity is an account that places emphasis on either memory, personality, or both. According to this view, our unique personalities, which are partially shaped by the memories of experiences we have had, make us who we are. This seems to be the best candidate for what the father of the 95472 family has in mind by "identity." Think of all of the ways that we come to be associated with numbers in our lives: we are assigned social security numbers, telephone numbers, and street addresses.

When information is collected for census purposes, we become nothing more than statistics. The real danger of this is that our identities—understood in terms of the personality characteristics and life experiences—are erased. This is problematic because people behave empathetically to other people, not to numbers.

That said, I'm not sure that 5's father employed the best strategy to make his point. His kids don't have developed story lines in the comic. They are, instead, kind of a one-off gag.

The Dust of Ancient Civilizations

The expression "cleanliness is next to godliness" is commonplace in our society. We've all heard it. The expression suggests that cleanliness is a virtue. Most people think that, all things being equal, we should keep our bodies and our living spaces as clean as possible. We think this for good reasons. If we keep clean, we are not as susceptible to germs that can make us, and those who live with us, ill.

It appears that Pigpen didn't get the memo. He is perpetually filthy. In fact, he is filthy so often, that when he's clean, his friends don't even recognize him. In his dirty state, the other children constantly berate him. Violet is disgusted by Pigpen and on a number of occasions she tries to wash him by dumping a bucket of water over his head.

Is cleanliness a virtue? If so, is it a virtue in all cases? Is it possible to care *too much* about cleanliness?

I don't know about you, but when Pigpen appears without his cloud of filth, to me, something feels wrong. I can't wait until he's dirty again. Perhaps you feel this way too. Why do we feel that way? If we all agree that it's generally good to be clean, why do we want Pigpen to be constantly dirty? If we think that cleanliness is a virtue, and the lack of it is a vice, why do we have the reaction that we do to Pigpen?

One obvious response is that we don't want the same things out of fictional characters that we want out of real people who live in the world. We don't want people to be serial killers, but we don't want characters like Hannibal Lecter or Freddy Krueger to change their ways. We want our villains to be bad to the bone. Though it may be true that we have different expectations out of fictional characters, I'm not sure that explains our reaction to Pigpen. It's not just that we think the gag is funny and we don't want to see it end. When Pigpen appears without his dust cloud, it seems like he isn't being true to himself.

Perhaps one of the reasons that we as readers and audience members want Pigpen to be constantly filthy has to do with our admiration for authenticity. We like people to express themselves—their *real* selves, in their actions. When Pigpen is clean, he simply isn't behaving authentically *as* Pigpen. He is allowing his behavior to be determined too much by the desires and expectations of his friends.

In Jean-Paul Sartre's famous work, *Being and Nothingness*, he talks about the various ways that people can fall into what he calls "bad faith." These are basically just ways in which people can fail to be authentic. All of them have to do with focusing too strongly on one aspect of our existence. So, for example, a person is in bad faith when they define themselves too much in terms of what Sartre calls their "facticity."

Your facticity is the group of unchangeable things that are true about you. Far example, your date and location of birth, the identity of your biological parents, and the socioeconomic circumstances in which you were raised are things that you can't change. You are inauthentic, however, if you think that these facts about yourself must define you forever. Just because you were born into certain socioeconomic conditions, it does not follow that you can't change your situation for the future.

Another way that you can fall into bad faith is to define yourself too much in terms of what Sartre calls your "transcendence." You can understand your transcendence as, basically, your possibilities for the future. Here's an example. Once, my family went on a float trip down the Green River on a raft. As is always true on these types of trips, we were on the raft with another group. The group we were paired with on this trip was a group of students who had just graduated from high school and were preparing to attend college in the fall. The river guide asked us all questions about what we did for a living. When he got to one of the students, the student said he was going to be pre-med in college and was then headed off to become a neurosurgeon. The guide was impressed and congratulated the boy repeatedly.

What was noteworthy about the exchange was that the student, when asked about himself, provided an account that included no facts that were currently true about him, and he was being congratulated for hard work that he had not yet done. If the student truly thought of himself in these terms, he was inauthentic, because he defined himself entirely in terms of what he might someday be, rather than in terms of what he is. Good faith requires striking the appropriate balance between facticity and transcendence.

The third way that a person can fall into bad faith is to define their character too strongly in terms of what other people think of them. We're constantly under the gaze of others in the community. When we think the opinions of others should dictate who we are, we're guilty of what Sartre calls "being for others." When we do this, again, we aren't really behaving like our authentic selves. And we value authenticity. This is why we don't want Pigpen to clean up his act, at least not for the sake of other people. If he cleans up, he's not behaving authentically.

There also may be more to the story. We might be at least a little misguided in our assessment of cleanliness as a virtue. Surely it's virtuous to *some* degree. But how can we determine just how much we should care about cleanliness?

The most famous philosopher to discuss the concept of virtue is Aristotle. His moral theory doesn't focus on the circumstances under which actions are good or bad. Rather, he focuses on the question of how people can develop good moral character. For Aristotle, good people will demonstrate virtues of character. To find out what the virtues of character look like, we need to find what he calls the "golden mean," which will exist somewhere between two extremes.

A crucial concept is the concept of moderation. Consider, for example, the virtue of courage. We find courage somewhere between cowardice and rashness. We can find the appropriate level of cleanliness in much the same way. If we care about cleanliness too much, we might sacrifice other important values. Parents who care too much about the cleanliness of their children's clothes might prevent those children from having important learning experiences that involve making a bit of a mess. On the other hand, if we don't care about cleanliness enough, we might get sick or lose track of important possessions.

So clearly, Pigpen could stand to be a little cleaner. However, even if cleanliness is a virtue, messiness is, perhaps, not always a vice. Pigpen's filth says something more about his character than simply his dislike for bathtubs. It also says something about the way he engages the world—he dives right in. He'll play in the mud puddles and he'll dig a hole to China in the sandbox. He doesn't let a fear of dirt and germs prevent him from really living in the world. This kind of curiosity is also a virtue. So, though Pigpen exemplifies failures with respect to some virtues, he exemplifies excellence in others.

A World of Pure Imagination

Like all schoolchildren, the kids in the *Peanuts* universe have very active imaginations. So do the animals. As a result, the strips contain not just kids, dogs, and birds, but also Kite-Eating Trees, Great Pumpkins, Red Barons, and Talking Cacti.

None of us can forget Snoopy's exploits as the World War I flying ace against his nemesis, The Red Baron. He is not the only character to participate in this fantasy. His faithful friend Woodstock often accompanies him on his imaginary journeys. Peppermint Patty's best friend Marcie also gets in on the act as "The French Lass" at the Moulin Rouge.

It seems that none of the characters are immune from belief in some type of fictional character. Linus believes in The Great Pumpkin, Lucy and Charlie Brown have experiences with the Kite-Eating Tree, and Spike (Snoopy's brother) maintains a close personal friendship with a Cactus that suffers from shoulder pain. What are we to make of these characters?

In the philosophical subfield of aesthetics, philosophers often discuss the ontological status of fictional characters.

What that means is that they discuss the kinds of things that fictional characters are, and the extent to which we can say that they actually exist. While no one maintains that fictional characters exist in the way that you or I do, they do seem to exist in some other sense.

The words "Charlie Brown" aren't just meaningless gibberish. They refer to someone. And the characteristics of that someone are reasonably fixed. Sadly, Charles Schulz passed away in 2000. As a result, any new additions to the universe won't be made by him. Should we count the changes made to the universe since his death as legitimate changes? Were the characters fully defined by the work of their creator?

As you've likely observed in other chapters of this book, some people were kind of frustrated with some of the happenings in *The Peanuts Movie* (2015), in which Charlie Brown is finally able to swallow his fear and talk to The Little Red-Haired Girl. Many viewers thought that this event changed the essential wishy-washy, anxiety-ridden nature of our dear protagonist too much. As a result, many people don't view Charlie Brown's triumph over his nerves in this case to be a real change to his character. They rule it out as a legitimate part of the *Peanuts* canon. This is true in the same way that people who write fan fiction about their favorite fictional characters don't actually change what is "true" about those characters.

These are all fascinating questions in their own right. But we can ask an even more "meta" set of questions about the *Peanuts* universe. We can ask about the status of the fictional creatures *within* the fictional universe. How are we to understand the status of characters like the Red Baron, the Great Pumpkin, the Kite Eating Tree, the School Building, and Spike's best friend, the Cactus?

Do the *Peanuts* characters occupy a magical universe? Do they live in a world in which inanimate objects *actually* come to life? Do trees, cacti, and school buildings *really* have active mental lives? Do they act on intentions? Or, instead, are we supposed to understand the actions of these characters as simply expressions of the over-active imaginations of a group of kindergarten kids and their dog?

There is evidence in both directions. Bricks actually fall from the school building when Sally is upset. The Kite-Eating Tree does consistently eat kites (and, on occasion, pianos). On the other hand, this type of behavior often comes to an abrupt end when someone else enters the panel or screen, which suggests that the whole thing has been imaginary. There is at least some reason to believe that, though all of the characters in the *Peanuts* universe are fictional, some characters are more fictional than others.

No End

This chapter really could go on and on. With 17,897 canonical strips, the *Peanuts* universe is vast. The list of *Peanuts* characters goes on and on, and Schulz was a pretty philosophical guy. *Peanuts* is replete with philosophical questions. For now, we'll reflect on these questions and look forward to discovering more every time we revisit the world of *Peanuts*.

References

Annas, Julia. 1993. *The Morality of Happiness*. Oxford University Press.
———. 2009. *Intelligent Virtue*. Oxford University Press.
Aristotle. 1984. *Nicomachean Ethics*. Oxford University Press.
Bateson, Gregory. 1979. *Mind and Nature: A Necessary Unity*. Dutton.
Beckett, Samuel. 1954. *Waiting for Godot*. Faber and Faber.
———. 2009. *Three Novels: Molloy, Malone Dies, The Unnameable*. Grove Press.
Bentham, Jeremy, 1996. *An Introduction to the Principles of Morals and Legislation*. Oxford University Press.
Bishop, Greg. 2015. How a Book on Stoicism Became Popular at Every Level in the NFL. *Sports Illustrated* <www.si.com/nfl/2015/12/08/ryan-holiday-nfl-stoicism-book-pete-carroll-bill-belichick>.
Brooks, Peter. 1992. *Reading for the Plot: Design and Intention in Narrative*. Harvard University Press.
Byrne, Rhonda. 2010 [2006]. *The Secret*. Atria.
Cain, Susan. 2013 [1012]. *Quiet: The Power of Introverts in a World that Can't Stop Talking*. Random House.
Camus, Albert. 1955. *The Myth of Sisyphus*. Vintage.
Caldwell, Christopher. 2015 [2000]. Against Snoopy. <www.ny-press.com/against-snoopy>.
Cicero, Marcus Tullius. 1960. *Cicero: Selected Works*. Penguin.
Czikszentmihalyi, Mihaly. 2008 [1990]. *Flow: The Psychology of Optimal Experience*. Harper Perennial.

References

Derrida, Jacques. 2008. *The Animal that Therefore I Am*. Fordham University Press.

Descartes, René. 1989. *The Passions of the Soul*. Hackett.

———. 2003. *Treatise of Man*. Prometheus.

———. 2007. From The Letters of 1646 and 1649. In Kalof and Fitzgerald 2007.

Detmer, David. 2008. *Sartre Explained: From Bad Faith to Authenticity*. Open Court.

Eco, Umberto. 1963. The World of Charlie Brown. Introduction to the first translated volume of *Peanuts* cartoon strips, *Arriva Charlie Brown!* English translation in Eco 1994.

———. 1964. *Apocalittici e Integrati* [Apocalyptic and Integrated Intellectuals]. Bompiani.

———. 1994. *Apocalypse Postponed*. Indiana University Press.

Foucault, Michel. 1988. *Madness and Civilization: A History of Insanity in the Age of Reason*. Vintage.

———. 2006 [1961]. *History of Madness*. Routledge.

Friedman, Marilyn. 1989. Friendship and Moral Growth. *Journal of Value Inquiry* 33:1.

Haybron, Daniel M. 2010. *The Pursuit of Unhappiness: The Elusive Psychology of Well-Being*. Oxford University Press.

Heidegger, Martin. 1969. *Discourse on Thinking*. Harper.

———. 2008 [1927]. *Being and Time*. Harper.

Herwitz, Daniel. 2008. *Aesthetics: Key Concepts in Philosophy*. Continuum.

Hippocrates. 2008. *The Law, Oath of Hippocrates, On the Surgery, and On the Sacred Disease*. Dodo.

Holiday, Ryan. 2014. *The Obstacle Is the Way: The Timeless Art of Turning Trials into Triumph*. Penguin.

Howard-Snyder, Daniel. 2016. Propositional Faith: What It Is and What It Is Not. In Rea and Pojman 2016.

Inge, M. Thomas, ed. 2000. *Charles M. Schulz: Conversations*. University Press of Mississippi.

Inwood, Brad, and Lloyd P. Gerson. 1998. *Hellenistic Philosophy: Introductory Readings*. Hackett.

Johnson, Rheta Grimsley. 1995 [1989]. *Good Grief: The Story of Charles M. Schulz*. Pharos.

Junkerjürgen, Ralf. 2009. *Haarfarben: Eine Kulturgeschichte in Europa seit der Antike*. Böhlau.

Kalof, Linda, and Amy Fitzgerald, eds. 2007. *The Animals Reader: The Essential Classic and Contemporary Writings*. Berg.

References

Kant, Immanuel. 1949. *Critique of Practical Reason and Other Writings in Moral Philosophy*. University of Chicago Press.

Keyes, C.L.M., and J. Haidt, eds. 2003. *Flourishing: Positive Psychology and the Life Well-Lived*. American Psychological Association.

Kierkegaard, Søren. 1980. *The Concept of Anxiety: A Simple Psychologically Orienting Deliberation on the Dogmatic Issue of Hereditary Sin*. Princeton University Press.

Kubzansky, Laura D., Rosalind J. Wright, Sheldon Cohen, S. Weiss, B. Rosner, and D. Sparrow. 2002. Breathing Easy: A Prospective Study of Optimism and Pulmonary Function in the Normative Aging Study. *Annals of Behavioral Medicine* 24:2.

Lacan, Jacques. 2009. *The Seminar of Jacques Lacan, Book V: The Formations of the Unconscious* <www.lacan.com/seminars1.htm#5>.

Lammers, Monica. 2016. Peanuts Cartoon Characters and Their Personality Disorders: Charlie Brown and His Friends. <https://reelrundown.com/animation/A-Psyche-Analysis-of-Charlie-Brown-and-his-Friends>.

Malamud, Randy. 2003. *Poetic Animals and Animal Souls*. Palgrave Macmillan.

Maruta, Toshiko, Robert C. Colligan, Michael Malinchoc, and K.P. Offord. 2000. Optimists vs Pessimists: Survival Rate Among Medical Patients Over a 30-Year Period. *Mayo Clinic Proceedings* 75.

Marwick, Arthur 2000. *The Sixties: Cultural Transformation in Britain, France, Italy, and the United States, c. 1958–c. 1974*. Oxford University Press.

McKenna, Erin. 2013. *Pets, People, and Pragmatism*. Fordham University Press.

Michaelis, David. 2007. *Schulz and Peanuts: A Biography*. HarperCollins.

Morris, Tom. 2004. *The Stoic Art of Living: Inner Resilience and Outer Results*. Open Court.

Nakamura, J. and Mihaly Csikszentmihalyi. 2003. The Construction of Meaning through Vital Engagement. In Keyes and Haidt 2003.

Nietzsche, Friedrich. 1994. *The Birth of Tragedy: Out of the Spirit of Music*. Penguin.

Plantinga, Alvin. 1993. *Warrant and Proper Function*. Oxford University Press.

References

Potts, Annie. 2007. The Mark of the Beast: Inscribing 'Animality' through Extreme Body Modification. In Simmons and Armstrong 2007.

Rea, Michael, and Louis P. Pojman, eds. 2014. *Philosophy of Religion: An Anthology*. Cengage Learning.

Riddel, Karen. 2016. Are Your Friends Really Your Friends? *Psychology Today* <www.psychologytoday.com/blog/friendship-observation/201606/are-your-friends-really-your-friends>.

Sartre, Jean-Paul. 2007 [1945]. *Existentialism Is a Humanism*. Yale University Press.

———. 2013 [1938]. *Nausea*. New Directions.

Schulz, Charles M. 2004–2016. *The Complete Peanuts*. Twenty-six volumes. Fantagraphics.

———. 2010. *My Life with Charlie Brown*. University Press of Mississippi.

Searle, John R. 1992. *The Rediscovery of the Mind*. MIT Press.

Simmons, Laurence, and Philip Armstrong, eds. 2007. *Knowing Animals*. Brill.

Stephens, William O., and Randolph Feezell. 2004. The Ideal of the Stoic Sportsman. *Journal of the Philosophy of Sport* 31.

Szasz, Thomas S. 1997 [1987]. *Insanity: The Idea and Its Consequences*. Syracuse University Press.

———. 2010 [1961]. *The Myth of Mental Illness: Foundations of a Theory of Personal Conduct*. Harper.

Bassano di Tufillo, Simona. 2010. *Piccola Storia dei Peanuts: Le Strisce Più Famose d'America tra Arte, Cultura, e Linguaggio*. Donzelli.

Tyler, Tom. 2009. The Case of the Camel. In Tyler and Rossini 2009.

Tyler, Tom, and Manuela Rossini, eds. 2009. *Animal Encounters*. Brill.

Vlastos, Gregory. 1991. *Socrates: Ironist and Moral Philosopher*. Cornell University Press.

Winnicott, Donald W. 1991 [1971]. *Playing and Reality*. Routledge.

———. 2011. *Reading Winnicott*. Routledge.

Uexküll, Jakob von. 2010. *A Foray into the Worlds of Animals and Humans: With a Theory of Meaning*. University of Minnesota Press.

Walker, A.D.M. 1978. The Ideal of Sincerity. *Mind* 87.

Wolf, Susan. 2012. *Meaning in Life and Why It Matters*. Princeton University Press.

Charlie Brown's All-Stars

CHELSI ARCHIBALD earned a Masters of Arts in English from Weber State University. She is a copy writer by day, creating web content for major corporate brands, and by night, like Charlie Brown, she contemplates the universe. While she resembles Peppermint Patty in appearance and relates to Lucy's assertive nature, she considers herself a kindred spirit with Linus due to his penchant for philosophizing and cuddling blankets.

JENNIFER BAKER is an associate professor of philosophy at the College of Charleston. She teaches and writes on ethical theory, in particular stoic ethical theory. Inspired by Lucy Van Pelt, she has put up a roadside stand that reads "Stoic Help, 5 cents" and "The Doctor is In." So far, it almost feels like potential clients are actively avoiding her. She's wondering if she should re-title the stand "Happiness, 5 cents."

MARIO BARILE is an Italian startupper in the field of service engineering. He has a background in communication and marketing, and has always been passionate about writing. When he was a child, he skived off school to watch *Peanuts* on TV, thinking it was not time wasted. Sooner or later, it all makes sense.

FERNANDO GABRIEL PAGNONI BERNS is professor at the Universidad de Buenos Aires. He is a PhD student and has published chapters in, among others, *Horrors of War: The Undead on the Battlefield*, edited by Cynthia Miller, *To See the Saw Movies: Essays on Torture Porn and Post 9/11 Horror*, edited by John

Wallis, *For His Eyes Only: The Women of James Bond*, edited by Lisa Funnell, and *Deconstructing Dads: Changing Images of Fathers in Popular Culture*, edited by Laura Tropp. Writing about popular culture is his security blanket. Sometimes it works and sometimes . . . not. Here, it worked.

JEFF CERVANTEZ is Assistant Professor of Philosophy at Crafton Hills College in Yucaipa, California. He received his PhD from the University of Tennessee, Knoxville. He has authored articles and made other academic contributions on various topics in the areas of political philosophy, ethics, and philosophy of religion. He is pretty sure that he is the real-life counterpart to Charlie Brown, only with more hair.

PETER COSTELLO is Professor of Philosophy and Public and Community Service at Providence College. He is the co-editor of *Phenomenology and the Arts* (forthcoming), author of *Layers in Husserl's Phenomenology* (2012) and editor of *Philosophy in Children's Literature* (2011). Peter often feels he sits with his elbows on a brick wall, talking about life with his friends. He has never, however, to his knowledge, been quoted in a sermon.

PATRICK CROSKERY is Associate Professor of Philosophy at Ohio Northern University. His primary work is in ethical theory and professional ethics, and his favorite way to engage students in ethical reasoning is have them compete in classroom versions of the Intercollegiate Ethics Bowl. He first encountered the ruthless efficiency of capitalism at the age of nine when he discovered that the manufacturer of his Snoopy astronaut doll did not bother to include the spot on Snoopy's back (sure, sure, it was hidden by the space suit . . .).

PAOLO DINI has a PhD in Aerospace Engineering from Penn State, in low-speed aerodynamics—so he understands some of the challenges faced by the Red Baron, and why baseballs have bumpy stitches. Since 2003 he has been a research fellow in the Department of Media and Communications at the London School of Economics, and much to his surprise has recently understood that money is not an object but a social relation of credit and debt.

VERENA EHRNBERGER is currently working as a legal expert and recently completed her Bachelor of Arts with a major in Literature and a minor in Philosophy in Vienna. Like Lucy she loves to hand out psychiatric advice and dreams of getting her own booth someday, which is why she started a Masters Program in Philosophy and Psychotherapy. She also blogs for TEDxVienna on a regular basis.

RICHARD GREENE is a Professor of Philosophy at Weber State University. He also serves as Executive Chair of the Intercollegiate Ethics Bowl. He's co-edited a number of books on pop culture and philosophy including *The Princess Bride and Philosophy: Inconceivable!*, *Dexter and Philosophy: Mind over Spatter*, *Quentin Tarantino and Philosophy: How to Philosophize with a Pair of Pliers and a Blowtorch*, and *The Sopranos and Philosophy: I Kill Therefore I Am*. He also self-identifies as a blockhead!

WM. CURTIS HOLTZEN identifies with Charlie Brown and has the life philosophy: "half empty or half full doesn't matter, someone is gonna knock it over." He holds a D.Th. from the University of South Africa and wishes people would stop asking him if he's ever been there (the answer is no). He is Professor of Philosophy and Theology at Hope International University, a place he has been to several times. While he is a *Simpsons* fanatic his wife and daughter are the true *Peanuts* fans, which is ironic since his wife has a deadly peanut allergy.

DANIEL LEONARD has been extra good this year, so he has a long list of credentials that he wants you to read: "Daniel has degrees from Boston University, the University of Leuven, and Wheaton College. He is the creator of *3eanuts*, a *Peanuts* remix website reviewed online by *Time*, *Entertainment Weekly*, and many others. Moreover, he also etc., etc." If it seems too complicated, make it easy on yourself: just send money. How about tens and twenties?

RACHEL ROBISON-GREENE is a PhD Candidate in Philosophy at UMass Amherst. She is co-editor of *The Golden Compass and Philosophy: God Bites the Dust*, *Boardwalk Empire and Philosophy: Bootleg This Book*, *Girls and Philosophy: This Book Isn't a Metaphor for Anything, Orange is the New Black and Philosophy: Last Exit from Litchfield*, and *The Princess Bride and Philosophy: Inconceivable!*. She has contributed chapters to *Quentin Tarantino and Philosophy*, *The Legend of Zelda and Philosophy*, *Zombies, Vampires, and Philosophy*, and *The Walking Dead and Philosophy*. Like Snoopy, Rachel enjoys sleeping on top of a doghouse!

HEIDI SAMUELSON is currently a Visiting Assistant Professor of Philosophy at Sweet Briar College in Virginia. She has written and presented on the overlap of philosophy and pop culture, particularly in platforms like stand-up comedy and comic books, usually through a lens of Foucauldian analysis or Critical Theory. Like Charlie Brown, she has spent many nights lying awake at night wondering "Why me?" "Why am I here?" and "Where did I go wrong?"

SEBASTIAN SCHUHBECK has degrees in English Studies, Theology, and Education Sciences from Ludwig Maximilians University in Munich, Germany. Instead of finishing his dissertation in medical ethics he has accepted the quite handsome monthly "bribery" that the state of Bavaria hands out to its high-school teachers. His school is Chiemgau-Gymnasium in Traunstein, Germany. He has written or co-authored books and articles on multimedia didactics in the classroom as well as Christian, Hindu, and Buddhist religion and philosophy. Much like Lucy he loves counseling people and could ideally do this for a living, but unfortunately his two daughters quite stubbornly refuse to pay him the five cents for each of his priceless pieces of advice.

WIELAND SCHWANEBECK teaches British literature and film at TU Dresden, Germany. He received a PhD in literary studies for an analysis of the impostor motif in the works of Patricia Highsmith, and he has edited or co-edited several books on literature, film, and masculinity studies. In the future, he'd like to compose more fiction, sitting on top of his doghouse, but he'd need to rent a whole pumpkin patch to store all the rejection letters.

JAMIE CARLIN WATSON is Assistant Professor of Philosophy at Broward College in Ft. Lauderdale, Forida. He writes on epistemology and expertise and is particularly interested in whether anyone can speak as an authority on morality. He attempted to interview Ms. Othmar on that topic, but he couldn't make out her answers. When he can sneak out of Florida in the fall, he can be found jumping in piles of leaves and wandering through pumpkin patches. He has also contributed chapters to *The Catcher in the Rye and Philosophy*, *The Princess Bride and Philosophy*, and *Discworld and Philosophy*.

Index

THE
PRINCESS
BRIDE
AND PHILOSOPHY
INCONCEIVABLE!

EDITED BY RICHARD GREENE AND
RACHEL ROBISON-GREENE